Register Your Book

We will send you new materials, lesson plans, and professional learning opportunities as they become available. Level up your classroom, and tap into the larger network of Center for Civic Education resources.

Date	Name

▷ civiced.org/ register-pc2-tg —— or scan ➔

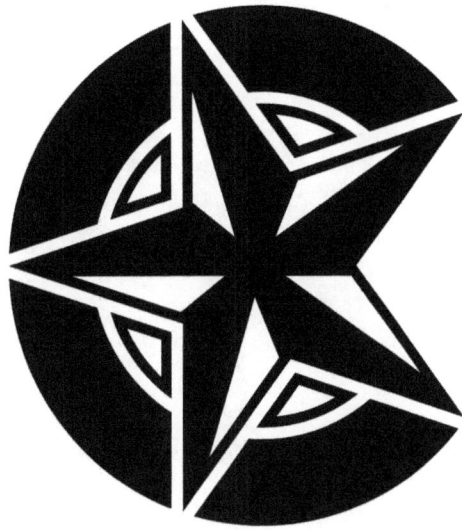

ProjectCitizen

Community Engagement in Public Policy

Level 2
Teacher's Guide

Administered by the Center for Civic Education

Project Citizen: Community Engagement in Public Policy is directed by the Center for Civic Education

For additional information, please contact the Center for Civic Education:
cce@civiced.org
www.civiced.org

26 25 24   01 02 03

First Edition   2007
Second Edition   2010
Third Edition   2024

ISBN-10:   0-89818-394-4
ISBN-13:   978-0-89818-394-8

A Note to Readers

Dear Educators,

We at the Center for Civic Education welcome your participation in *Project Citizen: Community Engagement in Public Policy*, a program for learning about public policy and making positive changes in your community. This text and program are designed to help showcase the importance of being involved in one's local community, state, and nation. It is an instructional tool that will help your students and participating community members learn the skills and knowledge they need to be active, responsible, and impactful citizens who help improve your community to ensure that everyone can enjoy their rights to life, liberty, property, and the pursuit of happiness.

New in this updated edition of Project Citizen are integrated opportunities, resources, and lessons for your students to learn and practice the skills of media literacy throughout the Project Citizen process. Understanding how to find sources, evaluate evidence, assess media credibility, and identify biases and misinformation are essential skills for everyone, especially those who are engaged in this project.

At the Center for Civic Education, we believe that the best way for people to build their civic knowledge, skills, and dispositions is by participating in democratic practices and community-based problem solving. We are all citizens of our own communities, and every member plays a vital role. We believe that all members of the community have a key role to play in making our communities strong and realizing our society's highest ambitions. With Project Citizen, you are on your way. We wish you well, and we look forward to seeing your community engagement in public policy!

Sincerely,

Dr. Donna Paoletti Phillips
President and Chief Executive Officer
Center for Civic Education

Acknowledgments

Project Citizen would not be alive today without the support and devotion of thousands of passionate educators across the country and around the world. Since 1993, Project Citizen has been taught in every state, the District of Columbia, and 88 countries with countless projects guiding students to deeper learning about public policy and their community. Through the years, scores of teachers have built an expertise in teaching Project Citizen and lent their hand to improving both the process and text. The names below are just some of the teacher experts who have given a portion of their time to improving this book. The Center is grateful for the helpful comments and suggestions received from the following persons who reviewed the manuscript in its various development stages. The Center has attempted to be responsive to the many valuable suggestions for improvement in the text. The final product, however, is the responsibility of the Center and does not necessarily reflect the views of those who have contributed their thoughts and ideas.

President and Chief Executive Officer

Dr. Donna Paoletti Phillips

Project Citizen Curriculum Team

Michael Blauw
Director of Civic Learning and Strategic Partnerships

Taja Butler
Manager of Civic Learning Projects

Kelly Reichardt
Manager of Civic Learning and Curriculum

Meghan Volcy
Coordinator of National Grant Projects

Director of Publishing and Communications

Mark Gage

Senior Designer and Editor

Bradford Pilcher

Project Citizen Evaluation Partner

Civic Engagement Research Lab
Georgetown University

Teacher's Guide Contributors

The following educators and content experts provided invaluable insight into the teaching of Project Citizen: Community Engagement in Public Policy and this teacher's guide reflects much of their instructional suggestions and advice. The final product, however, is the responsibility of the Center and does not reflect the views of those who have contributed their thoughts and ideas.

Stacy Walls Bartkowski
Teacher, Newark Charter High School
Newark, Delaware

Nathaniel Birkhead
Kansas State University,
Head, Department of Political Science, and
Distinguished Teaching Scholar
Manhattan, Kansas

Cheryl Cook-Kallio
California State Coordinator for We the People
and Project Citizen; Center for Civic Education
Board Member
Pleasanton, California

Dr. Francene Engel
Political Scientist,
Maryland Council for Civic and History Education
Annapolis, Maryland

Christine Hull
Program Director,
Nevada Center for Civic Engagement
Reno, Nevada

Jaclyn Jecha
Teacher, New Berlin West Middle and High School
New Berlin, Wisconsin

Leroy Smith, M.Ed.
Educational Consultant,
Realized Curriculum Solutions
Baltimore, Maryland

Lindsay Stepanek
Teacher, University High School
Morgantown, West Virginia

Kim Wahaus
Teacher, Olathe South High School
Olathe, Kansas

Contents

Instruction

OVERVIEW
OF PROJECT CITIZEN: COMMUNITY ENGAGEMENT IN PUBLIC POLICY, LEVEL 2

A Teacher's Guide Inquiry Approach

Project Citizen: Community Engagement in Public Policy has broad appeal in diverse contexts, including classrooms, after-school clubs, community and youth groups, and adult organizations. Those leading this program may be teachers, youth leaders, professors, or other types of facilitators. For simplicity, this text will use the terms *teacher* and *student(s)*, but know that these directions apply to anyone leading and implementing this program with others.

Suggested lesson plans for using the Project Citizen program, including the six-step Project Citizen process, are presented in this guide. Teachers are encouraged to follow the inquiry-based lesson plans to the extent they are useful in implementing Project Citizen and to adapt the suggestions as needed.

This program is grounded in an inquiry approach and thereby underscores the Educating for American Democracy (EAD) Pedagogy Companion's core principle of inquiry as a primary mode of learning. All chapters in Project Citizen, including the six steps in Chapter 3, are aligned to compelling and supporting questions, an approach aligned with the College, Career, and Civic Life (C3) Framework. The underlying structure of both the student project guide and the teacher's guide is based on the power of inquiry. Although the compelling and supporting question structure is not explicit in the project guide, this teacher's guide references the titles of each chapter of the project guide as

"compelling questions" and each subheading question found throughout the book as "supporting questions."

Project Citizen is largely an opportunity for students to ask, research, and answer their own important questions, which has strong alignment to Dimension 1 of the C3 Framework: Developing Questions and Planning Inquiries. Along the way, the inquiry approach in Project Citizen structures this process and allows students to apply disciplinary concepts (Dimension 2), evaluate sources and use evidence (Dimension 3), and communicate conclusions and take informed action (Dimension 4).

The pedagogy articulated in Project Citizen supports a process that prioritizes all students' voices and fosters active participation in their community engagement project as outlined in the EAD pedagogical principle of Excellence for All. These practices align with dispositional shifts outlined in the EAD. The culminating showcase in Project Citizen exemplifies EAD's pedagogical principles of Practice of Constitutional Democracy and Student Agency. Further alignment between both the C3 Framework and the EAD Roadmap are outlined in this Overview.

This teacher's guide will give further suggestions and strategies to support all learners, as well as ways to anchor student learning more deeply through inquiry. There are many optional and adaptable student and teacher resources in this guide that can be used alongside those already found in the project guide.

Each suggested lesson in this guide is anchored by compelling and supporting questions and follows the 5E Instructional Model, a pedagogical framework used to immerse students in the process of inquiry-based learning. The model consists of five phases: Engage, Explore, Explain, Elaborate, and Evaluate. Within the inquiry arc of the compelling questions, the 5E Instructional Model promotes active engagement, critical thinking, and collaborative learning, fostering a deeper and more meaningful understanding of concepts. Applied to Project Citizen, the 5E Model is a follows:

- **Engage:** Each new chapter kicks off with a question to activate students' prior knowledge. Note that this is distinct from background knowledge. Prior knowledge is connected to student experiences and prior conceptual understandings of the themes, concepts, or topics. For example, the concepts of

community and how students know when something should be changed are ideas that students can grapple with that will prime them for the learning to follow in Project Citizen.

- **Explore:** Using the student project guide, students access and explore new ideas from sources in the text. The project guide includes activities that allow them to do this in meaningful and collaborative ways. The teacher's guide will include additional suggestions for differentiation and adaptation.

- **Explain:** In inquiry, "explain" signifies a time for students to share their learning, not for teachers to lecture. In Project Citizen, this will include embedded activities throughout the text for students to check their understanding and for teachers to clarify misunderstandings. This is a great way for the class to check in on each other's developing knowledge and to support all students' learning.

- **Elaborate:** Using the activities in the project guide and the teacher's guide, students begin to synthesize and apply their thinking. Embedded activities, such as Making Connections and Collaborate Together, support this phase of inquiry. In preparation for the final Project Citizen showcase, this phase is used along the way. Additionally, in the larger inquiry arc of Project Citizen, this phase includes the simulated public hearing, which is Step 5.

- **Evaluate:** Checking for understanding throughout the Project Citizen process is essential. The project guide and the teacher's guide both include many options for doing so. These formative assessments allow teachers to decide on the next best steps for student learning. The "evaluate" for Project Citizen is also the reflection students do at the end of the entire process in Step 6.

The lessons in this teacher's guide also give the teacher suggestions for a "whole-class project" and "small-group projects." The teacher may elect to have the entire class work on one public policy problem, or the teacher might want students to work in groups, each selecting a different public policy problem.

Additionally, throughout the student project guide are opportunities to apply the skills of media literacy to civic learning. These will be noted in-line with the overall inquiry guidance in each chapter. There are additional robust opportunities for teachers to deepen student learning in media literacy through full 5E inquiry lessons available in this guide. Teachers are encouraged to preview these and decide how and when to extend student learning on this essential civic skill during the course of their instruction. A full correlation chart of the integrated media-literacy skills is included and full media-literacy lessons that can be implemented along with Project Citizen or used as standalone lessons are included in this guide.

B Rationale and Goals of Project Citizen

Purpose

Every person is part of a community. No matter who they are or how old they are, their community has an impact on them, and importantly, they have an impact on their community. Communities are powerful not only because they often give us a sense of identity and purpose but also because they also help us solve problems.

This project guide is about how students can use the power of their community to solve problems through public policy. Public policy is an agreed-upon way that our government fulfills its responsibilities and solves problems.

A Note on the Term Citizen

Project Citizen: Community Engagement in Public Policy is first and foremost a process for conducting a community project in public policy. Any member of a community can partake in such a project!

It is first important to acknowledge the term *citizen* in the student project guide's title and its use throughout the student text. The broader definition of *citizen* means any active and responsible participant in any community or group. This broad civic use of the word contrasts with its narrower use in reference to individuals with full rights and privileges under a particular system of government.

Citizenship in its narrower sense can often imply a legal or social status that grants

individuals privileges, such as the right to vote. Citizenship in its broader sense, however, often refers to the basic rights and responsibilities that any resident can enjoy by participating in the civic life of a community or country. This form of citizenship emphasizes the everyday actions and behaviors of individuals engaging in community activities. Not everyone has the legal status of citizen, nor does everyone have the possibility of becoming one, but everyone is a neighbor, has individual rights, and can be a contributing member of the body of a community. Civic engagement is not just about electoral politics—it is about what we do and how we conduct ourselves in a community.

American history is full of examples of individuals and groups who made monumental impacts on their communities and countries without the status and privileges of legally recognized citizenship. For example, the movement to abolish slavery, the movement for women's suffrage, and the civil rights movements of Black and Indigenous Americans were all largely powered by those who did not have the right to vote. Young people, who were not yet old enough to vote, also used public policy and the American political system to lower the voting age to 18 through the 26th Amendment. And labor movements, such as those led by the United Farm Workers, were driven by people who were not necessarily citizens in the legal sense, but who were able to use their First Amendment rights of speech, assembly, and petition to influence public policy.

Our government has a tradition of citizenship in the broader sense. Project Citizen is intended to strengthen the knowledge, skills, and habits of this type of citizenship.

The Student's Role in the American Political System

Because the United States is a constitutional democracy, most decision making and other work of government is accomplished by elected and appointed representatives.

Since the founding of our nation, however, the preservation and healthy functioning of our democracy requires that community members—or *citizens*, as we refer to them from now on—play an active role in what is ultimately a system of self-government. For citizens to play such a role requires, among other things, that they

- understand their system of government;
- have the knowledge, skills, and willingness to participate to an adequate degree;
- participate guided by an enlightened, reasoned commitment to the fundamental values and principles of American democracy; and
- understand the limits of government.

The principal purpose of Project Citizen is to help students improve their capacities to participate competently and responsibly in the American political system. In addition to the requirements noted above, such participation requires that students have the ability to keep track of, or monitor, what their government is doing and to influence it on matters of concern to them.

In a country as large and complex as the United States, monitoring and influencing government is not always an easy task. Our system of government follows a federal structure where powers are shared among multiple levels of government. It includes three branches of government—legislative, executive, and judicial—each at national, state, local, and tribal governments, as well as tens of thousands affiliated agencies. This system is challenging to citizens, who are often confused about which level or levels of government and which branches or agencies of government are responsible for matters of interest to them.

Project Citizen provides a practical, project-based approach to learning about our complex system of government and how to monitor and influence it. As an important note, most of this book is geared toward students in a classroom setting, and the language often reflects that. Since Project Citizen is for everyone, however, know that the group you are leading can take part in the Project Citizen process, even if they are not students and even if they are conducting the project outside the classroom. In any case, they will work together with others to conduct research in their community in order to discover problems that they think their governments are not handling well or not handling at all. Then they will select a problem from among those identified and work cooperatively to

- conduct research on a community problem;
- evaluate alternative—different or various kinds of—solutions to the problem and weigh their advantages and disadvantages;

- propose a solution to the problem that requires governmental action and does not violate provisions of their state and federal constitutions; and
- propose an engagement plan to influence the appropriate governmental agencies to consider or adopt their proposed solution to the problem.

Once these tasks are completed, students record the results of their work in a portfolio. Then they participate in a simulated public hearing in which they present the results of their work to a panel of public- and/or private-sphere representatives from their community. If your class wishes to do so, you may also actively try to get government officials to consider or adopt the solutions to problems they have proposed.

By taking part in Project Citizen, your students will learn by doing the work of active citizens in their community and will learn

- about the existence and roles of *civil society*—the sphere of voluntary activity in society—in the political process;
- which branches, agencies, and levels of government have the authority and responsibility to deal with the problem they have chosen; and
- how to monitor and influence the political process in their community, state, or nation.

Although your students' attention may have been limited to one particular problem in their community or state, the knowledge and skills they gain are those required for competent and responsible participation throughout the American political system.

The hope of Project Citizen is that the experiences and learning it fosters will encourage your students to take an active role in the political life of their community, state, and nation for the rest of their lives. If the United States is to fulfill its mission of being a nation of, by, and for the people, dedicated to liberty and justice for all, it is essential that the people take part in their system of self-government.

C Media Literacy in Project Citizen

Opportunities to develop media literacy, meaning skills to critically analyze and evaluate the information presented in media sources, including newspapers, television, radio, and digital platforms, are integrated throughout the six Project Citizen steps. Educators may choose to deepen their learning in media literacy even further along the way. The chart below highlights the opportunities you will have to integrate media literacy as you successfully pursue your Project Citizen goals with your students. Additionally, information about eight full, inquiry-based media-literacy lessons aligned to the media-literacy topics and compelling questions in this chart can be found in Appendix C.

Chapter	Project Citizen Topics	Media Literacy Moments
1	Do I Have the Power to Create Change in My Community?	● Does a Free Press Support Democracy?
2	Do We Need Public Policy?	
3	How Does Project Citizen Empower My Engagement in Public Policy?	● Do I Have a Role in Media Literacy?
	Step 1: Identifying Problems to Be Dealt With by Public Policy	● Do Different Types of Media Shape Community Perspectives on Public Issues?
	Step 2: Selecting a Problem or Problems for Your Class to Study	
	Step 3: Gathering Information on the Problem You Will Study	● Is All Media Biased? ● Can I Identify Reliable Media Sources? ● Do I Play a Role in Staying Safe Online? ● Do I Have to Cite My Sources?
	Step 4: Developing a Portfolio to Present Your Research	● Can I Effectively Create and Share Information?
	Step 5: Presenting Your Portfolio in a Simulated Public Hearing	
	Step 6: Reflecting on Your Experience	● Am I Media Literate?
4	Why Is My Participation Important to Democracy?	

D Research and Evaluation on Project Citizen

Research on Project Citizen, both in the United States and in other countries, has shown that students who participate in the program become skilled at monitoring public policy and participating in its development. Students are better able to communicate effectively with local authorities, gather information from a wide variety of sources, and persuade others to support their positions. Students acquire participatory skills, such as identifying and effectively communicating with public officials and attending and making presentations at meetings of governmental agencies, such as city councils. Students come to conceive of themselves as *participatory* citizens. They express greater confidence in their knowledge about local government and test higher on levels of political knowledge. In more than half of Project Citizen classes, students have gone beyond the requirements of the program by attempting to get their governments to implement their proposals. Many local government officials have expressed appreciation of students' efforts and see them as partners in improving the quality of life of their communities.

The Georgetown University Civic Education Research Lab (CERL) researched the effectiveness of the Center's Project Citizen program, sharing their insights in the "Project Citizen Research Program 2024 Report."[1] The research for this report was unique in its rigor as a randomized control trial study.

Over three academic years, from 2020 to 2023, they examined how the program impacted both middle and high school students and their teachers. The results of the evaluation revealed significant positive effects for both students and teachers in the focus areas of civic knowledge, civic dispositions, civic skills, civic engagement, competencies related to social-emotional learning (SEL), and science, technology, engineering, and math (STEM) skills.[2] Student participants experienced notable increases in their understanding of civic knowledge, confidence in civic engagement, and interest in pursuing careers in government service. They also demonstrated enhanced problem-solving abilities and a greater sense of efficacy in effecting change within their communities.

For teachers, the program included participating in professional development consisting of a summer workshop and ongoing mentored sessions throughout the school year. Students involved in the

---

[1] Diana Owen, "Project Citizen Research Program 2024 Report," ResearchGate, 2024, https://www.researchgate.net/publication/378867385_PCRP_Final_Report.

[2] "Project Citizen Shows Significant Impact on Teachers and Students," Civic Education Research Lab, 2024, https://cerl.georgetown.edu/news/project-citizen-shows-significant-impact-on-teachers-and-students/.

program engaged in collaborative research, policy development, and presentations on a policy problem in their school or community. Teachers reported feeling more connected to civic education and observed improvements in their ability to teach civic skills. They also integrated civic activities more frequently into their lessons and felt more effective in encouraging student involvement in community issues. Furthermore, the program fostered the development of SEL competencies, such as collaboration, social awareness, and responsible decision making among students, and there was a notable increase in the use of STEM skills in addressing community problems.[3]

In a time when civic education and engagement are crucial, Project Citizen shows promise in engaging students in their education and communities, keeping teachers energized and supported through robust professional development, and producing informed, empowered participants in democracy.

---

[3] Meghan Volcy, "April 2024 Research Impact: Project Citizen," Center for Civic Education, 2024, https://civiced.org/research-impact-april-2024.

E Project Citizen and Service Learning

In service learning, students learn educational standards through tackling real-life problems in their community. This makes service learning and Project Citizen a natural fit for each other. Many of the goals of service learning and Project Citizen are mutually reinforcing. In fact, Project Citizen is a convenient method for meeting service-learning criteria as outlined in many states for their Civic Seals of Excellence. These seals are often a way of recognizing and incentivizing student civic engagement. Though these criteria vary across states and are constantly changing, see below for some of the best practices for school-based service learning[4] and how they align with Project Citizen:

1. **Meeting a recognized need in the community**
   Project Citizen students explore a variety of real public policy problems or issues. As a class, they select one problem for in-depth study. Students formulate a public policy to address the problem and develop an engagement plan for having their policy implemented by an appropriate governing body or agency.

2. **Achieving curricular objectives through service learning**
   Project Citizen is an ideal project for an interdisciplinary core program or for social studies and language arts, or STEM classes. The content and instructional approach used in the program helps ground service learning in the core curriculum.

3. **Reflecting throughout the service learning experience**
   As students complete the various tasks involved in developing a class or group portfolio, they must reflect upon the nature and extent of the public policy problem they are working on, the potential of their proposed policy to solve the problem, and the impact that their proposed policy would have on the community and themselves. Project Citizen culminates with students reflecting on the entire learning experience.

---

[4] Adapted from *Maryland Student Service-Learning Guidelines* (Baltimore: Maryland State Department of Education), revised 2019.

4. **Developing student responsibility**
   Throughout the program, students are assigned specific individual and group responsibilities that they must fulfill to complete the portfolio and prepare for the simulated hearing. Working in teams helps prepare them for taking on responsibilities associated with service-learning assignments.

5. **Establishing community partnerships**
   In researching their problem and preparing policy, students contact public officials, community leaders and experts, and businesspeople. These contacts help develop working relationships with government agencies, community groups, and other organizations that can assist schools with their service-learning program.

6. **Planning ahead for service learning**
   The contacts that students make during their research enables them to select service-learning assignments that are consistent with the other characteristics of effective service learning. Service-learning assignments will be intentional and organized if students participate in the identification of projects they want to undertake and stay true to the steps of the Project Citizen process.

7. **Equipping students with the knowledge and skills needed for service**
   In addition to teaching students how to monitor and influence public policy and increasing their knowledge about their community, Project Citizen helps students develop oral and written communication skills, research skills, and interpersonal skills. Project Citizen also helps students develop civic attitudes essential for engagement.

F Project Citizen Alignment to National Frameworks and Roadmaps

College, Career, and Civic Life (C3) Framework

Chapter	Project Citizen Compelling Questions	College, Career, and Civic Life Framework
1	Do I Have the Power to Create Change in My Community?	**Dimension 1:** Developing Questions and Planning Inquiries **Dimension 2:** Applying Disciplinary Tools and Concepts (Civics, History)
2	Do We Need Public Policy?	**Dimension 2:** Applying Disciplinary Tools and Concepts (Civics, History)
3	How Does Project Citizen Empower My Engagement in Public Policy?	
	Step 1: Identifying Problems to Be Dealt With by Public Policy	**Dimension 1:** Developing Questions and Planning Inquiries
	Step 2: Selecting a Problem or Problems for Your Class to Study	**Dimension 3:** Evaluating Sources and Using Evidence
	Step 3: Gathering Information on the Problem You Will Study	**Dimension 3:** Gathering and Evaluating Sources
	Step 4: Developing a Portfolio to Present Your Research	**Dimension 3:** Developing Claims and Using Evidence
	Step 5: Presenting Your Portfolio in a Simulated Public Hearing	**Dimension 4:** Communicating and Critiquing Conclusions
	Step 6: Reflecting on Your Experience	**Dimension 4:** Communicating and Critiquing Conclusions
4	Why Is My Participation Important to Democracy?	**Dimension 4:** Taking Informed Action

Educating for American Democracy (EAD) Roadmap

EAD Overarching Themes:
Theme 1: Civic Participation
Theme 7: A People with Contemporary Debates and Possibilities

EAD Design Challenges (DC):
DC1: Motivating Agency, Sustaining the Republic
DC3: Simultaneously Celebrating and Critiquing Compromise

Pedagogy Companion Principle #4: Inquiry as the Primary Mode of Learning

Chapter	Project Citizen Compelling Questions	EAD Roadmap and Pedagogy Companion
1	Do I Have the Power to Create Change in My Community?	**Pedagogy Companion Principle #1:** Excellence for All; "Relevance, rigor, and relationship"
2	Do We Need Public Policy?	**DC1.1:** How can we help students understand the full context of their role as citizens and civic participants without creating paralysis or a sense of the insignificance of their own agency in relation to the magnitude of our society, the globe, and shared challenges?
3	How Does Project Citizen Empower My Engagement in Public Policy?	**DC3.1:** How can we help students make sense of the paradox that Americans continuously disagree about the ideal shape of self-government but also agree to preserve shared institutions?
	Step 1: Identifying Problems to Be Dealt With by Public Policy	**DC1.2:** How can we help students become engaged citizens who also sustain civil disagreement, civic friendship, and this American constitutional democracy?

Chapter	Project Citizen Compelling Questions	EAD Roadmap and Pedagogy Companion
	Step 2: Selecting a Problem or Problems for Your Class to Study	**Pedagogy Companion Principle #1:** Excellence for All; community building **Pedagogy Companion Principle #2:** Growth Mindset and Capacity Building; "Reflect, relearn, revise, and revisit" **Pedagogy Companion Principle #3:** Building an EAD-Ready Classroom and School; student voice and leadership, parent and community connection, inclusive culture **Parents'/caregivers'** role as student civic project partners
	Step 3: Gathering Information on the Problem You Will Study	
	Step 4: Developing a Portfolio to Present Your Research	**Pedagogy Companion Principle #5:** Practice of Constitutional Democracy and Student Agency; project-based learning (PBL), authentic writing/media tasks, classroom deliberation
	Step 5: Presenting Your Portfolio in a Simulated Public Hearing	**DC1.3:** How can we help students pursue civic action that is authentic, responsible, and informed? **Pedagogy Companion Principle #5:** Practice of Constitutional Democracy and Student Agency; PBL, civic engagement projects leading to informed action, showcases and competitions
	Step 6: Reflecting on Your Experience	**Pedagogy Companion Principle #5:** Practice of Constitutional Democracy and Student Agency; PBL, authentic writing/media tasks
4	Why Is My Participation Important to Democracy?	**Pedagogy Companion Principle #3:** Building an EAD-Ready Classroom and School; student voice and leadership

BEFORE YOU START
SUGGESTIONS FROM TEACHERS

Project Citizen To-Do List

1. **Integrate Project Citizen into your daily and unit planning:** Use the overview and outline of Project Citizen to determine how to best integrate it into your curriculum. Use the inquiry lessons in this guide as a basis to plan full and mini lessons to teach students specific skills and knowledge they need at each step in the project. Modify and adapt the Project Citizen lessons and materials to best meet the needs of your students and the demands of your curriculum goals. Lesson plans are provided in this guide, which you may need to adapt or supplement to meet your students' unique needs.

2. **Align Project Citizen to your standards or objectives and identify your main goal:** You should identify your main goal before beginning this project. For example, if your main goal is increasing general civic knowledge, you will plan to spend more time on the introductory lessons about the U.S. political system and public policy than on teamwork. Or if your main goal is for students to enhance their research, media literacy, and writing skills, you will spend more time in those areas.

3. **Create a timeline:** See the suggested timelines in the next section, adapt them to your teaching context, or make your own.

4. **Create as many democratic opportunities as possible for students to participate in the project:**

   A. **Create structure and individual accountability** for students by giving them a timeline at the beginning of the project and sticking to it, having daily mini lessons and daily debriefings, and letting students know that their grade depends on their mastery of each step in Project Citizen; check for completion of daily assignments.

   B. **Provide ample opportunity for students to choose** group members, the problem they study, the format they use for their portfolios, whom they present to, etc.

   C. **Prioritize practice, feedback, and reflection.** Schedule enough time during the project for students to learn from and grow with each other through peer feedback, revision, and reflection. This is where the learning sinks in!

   D. **Provide an opportunity for a public hearing.** This will help motivate students to produce high-quality work of which they can be proud. This is the most memorable, empowering, and rewarding part of the whole experience.

E. Model civil discourse and approach local issues with sensitivity, teach students how to propose policy changes without making individuals feel attacked, and avoid deluging public officials with multiple requests for the same information.

5. **Establish grading practices for Project Citizen:** There are many ways to assess students' acquisition of the knowledge and skills you want them to gain through Project Citizen. Teachers can create a list of requirements that each student must meet and that you will assess. Beyond the project portfolio itself, there are various resources and activities within the student project guide that lend themselves to assessing student learning. These resources are labeled in the project guide as follows:

A. Graphic Organizer
B. Student Reflection
C. Collaborate Together
D. Making Connections
E. Media Literacy Moments
F. Resource

Additionally, there are suggestions for assessing group work, research, and media-literacy skills throughout the teacher's guide. Also take note that the Project Citizen Portfolio and Hearing Evaluation Sheet is included in the appendix of this book and in the project guide. This resource is designed to assist you and community evaluators in evaluating students' work and their presentations. The criteria also provide you with the elements you need for summative assessment of the project.

6. **Contact community leaders:** Use the Community Leader Message template provided in the appendix to solicit the participation of community leaders. Note that this message is most often sent via email, though hard-copy letters are still an option. You may also alter the communication or write your own message to ask community leaders to participate in your students' Project Citizen experience. This is a great way to gain support from the community. It is important to circulate this message early in the process to allow interested leaders enough time to arrange their schedules so they can be available at the appropriate time.

7. **Schedule final presentations:** You should set an end date for the project and schedule the final presentation in the form of a simulated public hearing. This can serve as a powerful motivator. Also, it is important to get on the agendas for public meetings or reserve space in meeting rooms or another venue. Setting a date for final presentations early is also helpful for scheduling evaluators.

Establishing a Timeline and Planning for Classroom Implementation

The format and timeline for teaching Project Citizen can vary greatly across schools, districts, and states. There are as many unique timelines and structures for teaching Project Citizen as there are teachers using the program. Some veteran Project Citizen teachers have gone as far as claiming that the curriculum is like jello—it can fit into whatever mold you need. Below are some suggested timings to consider.

Consolidated Timing

Four weeks is ample time to do Project Citizen as the primary focus for instruction. Many secondary teachers use a four-week timeframe and have found success. Teachers who feel that they do not have time in their year for another project of this scale should note that Project Citizen is a comprehensive curriculum on civic engagement. Therefore, it may be used in place of, not in addition to, other curricula on this topic. Because of the depth of research and the authenticity of the final presentation, students and teachers often find that the reading, writing, speaking, and listening skills honed during the project make it a worthy investment in time. Many teachers have also found that Project Citizen can be used in place of other strategies to sharpen these same skills. While four weeks is ample time, many teachers report that a six- to nine-week block of class time is more ideal for a rewarding Project Citizen experience.

Sample Timelines

The following sample timelines are based on a secondary schedule with classes meeting with five 45-minute classes a week or the equivalent time in a block schedule. Teachers should note that Step 3 is often the most time-consuming element of the program. This step includes the lengthy process of gathering relevant and appropriate information from multiple sources, analyzing and organizing the information gathered, and the physical construction of the four components of the portfolio display and the documentation assembly. These steps constitute the heart of Project Citizen and must be given adequate time to ensure success. Between the following two suggested pacing schedules, teachers can find variations and adaptations that work best for their timing.

If You Have Four Weeks

- Week 1: Chapters 1–2; Steps 1–2 in Chapter 3 (introduction to Project Citizen, foundational principles, public policy, and the identification and selection of a problem for study)
- Week 2: Steps 3–4 in Chapter 3 (problem research, analysis and organization of information, and developing the portfolio)
- Week 3: Step 4 in Chapter 3 (completion of the four portfolio tasks)
- Week 4: Steps 5–6 in Chapter 3; Chapter 4 (presenting in a public hearing and reflecting on the learning and experience)

If You Have Eight Weeks

- Week 1: Chapters 1–2 (introduction to Project Citizen, foundational principles, and public policy)
- Week 2: Chapter 3, Steps 1–2 (identifying public policy problems in the community and selecting a problem for study)
- Week 3: Step 3 (gathering information on the problem from multiple sources)
- Week 4: Step 3 (continuing to gather, analyze, and organize the information)
- Week 5: Step 4 (class discussion and planning of the four components of the portfolio)
- Week 6: Step 4 (small-group work for completion of the four components of the portfolio)
- Week 7: Step 5 (practice and presentation of the portfolio in a simulated or actual public hearing)
- Week 8: Step 6; Chapter 4 (reflection on the learning and experience)

Creative Integration of Project Citizen

Teachers with more curricular or time restraints have been creative in their implementation of Project Citizen. For example, some teachers have created "Project Citizen Days" every Friday throughout their annual calendar where students work on a project over the course of a year or semester. Other teachers have used the first two chapters of Project Citizen in conjunction with another of their curricular units, and then turn to the more-involved project-oriented steps in Chapter 3 after state or Advanced Placement testing in order to form a kind of end-of-year/term capstone project. There is no one perfect way to implement Project Citizen, and there are as many ways of implementing Project Citizen as there are teachers.

Suggestions for Group Work and Cooperative Learning

Project Citizen provides an opportunity for students to improve their civic participation skills by working in groups to accomplish a common goal. How you structure the groups within your class will depend on factors such as total class size, academic achievement level of the students, and specific group dynamics. The following models are suggestions that have worked well for many teachers in the past. You may adapt these to fit your specific circumstances and to create a productive, cooperative-learning environment for all students.

Regardless of which of the following group models you choose, it is recommended that teachers guide all students through Chapters 1 and 2 and Chapter 3, Steps 1–3 of Project Citizen together before they break into portfolio task groups to create their portfolio. It is important that each student participates in developing each of the four main tasks: explaining a problem, evaluating different policies dealing with the problem, developing a policy to deal with the problem, and developing an engagement action plan designed to influence policymakers to adopt the proposed policy. Only after students have worked together on each of these tasks should they be divided into four portfolio groups—each assigned to develop one part of the class portfolio addressing one of the four main tasks identified above. Conducting a whole-class project on one community problem, if possible, can be transformational for the development of civic dispositions. A whole-class project is one aspect of this program that differentiates Project Citizen from others. If you do have students work on different problems in smaller groups, however, students will still benefit from the Project Citizen experience.

Whole-Class Project

In this model, all students in a class work on the same problem. Work is divided among portfolio groups to create the final class portfolio. This model emphasizes consensus building and teamwork. It is ideal for smaller classes and groups who benefit from more support in their research and writing skills (e.g., younger students, English language learners, and students with special needs).

Benefits
- It creates strong class unity.
- There are multiple opportunities for whole-class discussion, instruction, and debate.
- The teacher is able to make more specific and targeted suggestions, help with research, and steer the entire project.

- Higher-level research is produced when all students research the same topic, lending itself to better media-literacy opportunities.
- Simulated hearings or authentic presentations are easier to schedule.
- It teaches principles and values associated with participation in a constitutional democracy.

Drawbacks
- It may take longer to reach consensus on which problem to study and a class policy proposal.
- The teacher will possibly need to navigate disappointment due to students' topics not being chosen.
- More differentiation is needed to keep all students actively involved and individually accountable for work.
- Large classes (more than 20 students) end up with large portfolio task groups (more than five students per group).

If you choose this model, look for tips throughout this guide under the heading "Whole-Class Project."

Small-Group Projects
In this model, a large class is divided into smaller groups—as few as two groups will do—that each study a different problem and produce their own portfolios. This model is best suited for more academically advanced students and larger classes. This model emphasizes individual accountability and student choice.

Groups May Be Formed in a Number of Ways
A recommended method for creating productive groups is to have students work individually on Chapters 1 and 2 and Step 1 in Chapter 3. This encourages students to monitor public policy issues that they individually care about before choosing their group members. In Step 2: Selecting a Problem or Problems for Your Class to Study, you help students find others in the class who have similar policy interests. Students are encouraged to form groups based on common policy interests rather than established friendships.

Alternatively, you may assign students to work in heterogeneous groups to ensure that all groups have members with various strengths to contribute. You may also allow students to choose their groups first, then require each group to reach consensus on a problem to study.

Benefits
- Students are able to choose the problem they study, whom they work with, and many elements of the project—this creates buy-in for most students.
- Individual student accountability may be greater.
- Students learn about a number of policy issues from other students' presentations.
- Group sizes in classrooms of any size are manageable.

Drawbacks
- There is less teacher oversight of each group's progress and little room for teacher suggestions on specific research sources.
- Scheduling hearings and presentations for multiple groups is more difficult than scheduling for one large group.
- There is less depth of research when fewer students research the same topic.
- The entire class does not form team spirit together, although small groups do.
- It is more logistically challenging for the teacher to manage the four components for multiple projects.

If you choose this model, look for tips throughout this guide under the heading "Small-Group Projects."

Using Volunteers and Community Resources

Engaging Volunteers

It is highly recommended that teachers and students ask volunteers to assist students with the tasks necessary to develop the class portfolio. Volunteers may be parents, senior citizens, teacher aides, youth organization leaders, community leaders, or other civic-minded people. Volunteers may share real-life experiences in the application of the ideas under consideration, serve as guest speakers, enrich field experiences by serving as guides, and establish ongoing relationships with the class. Volunteers should be available regularly, either virtually or in person, to respond to questions or issues that may arise during the program.

Analyzing Public Policy Problems of Local Concern

Volunteers who are members of local politically active groups can help raise student awareness of public policy problems that are being debated in your community. Invite members from civic organizations, nonprofits, or politically active groups to talk to your students in the early stages of the policy-analysis process (in Chapter 3, Step 1 or 2) to help raise student awareness of the range of problems to study.

Members of Your State and Local Government

State and local officials can provide helpful information to assist students. They can provide deep insight into a class's research, knowledge of local problems, and understanding of public policy, as well as the realities of implementing public policy. Local elected officials are often eager to engage with students in civic education,

and most teachers who contact the officials' offices are surprised at how amenable they are to communicating with students. When decision makers are not available, their staff can often be equally helpful.

Take note, however, that some states, districts, and schools have passed public policy to limit student engagement with elected officials or government offices. As with many aspects of Project Citizen, often the most valuable engagement happens at the most local level, so in such cases, consider communicating with staffers, unelected officials, or other subject-matter experts at the hyper-local level. Remember, **engaging with government officials or any community volunteers is not a requirement of Project Citizen.** Most teachers have simply found that these real-world connections to the community deeply enrich student learning and their overall civic experience.

INSTRUCTION

1 Do I Have the Power to Create Change in My Community?

Purpose

Every person is part of a community. No matter who you are, or how old you are, your community has an impact on you, and importantly, you have an impact on your community. Communities are powerful not only because they often give us a sense of identity and purpose, but also because they also help us solve problems.

This first chapter explains the Project Citizen: Community Engagement in Public Policy program and the meaning behind citizenship and civic engagement in your community. It also provides descriptions of five democratic concepts that are useful to understanding the American political system. When you have finished this chapter, students should be able to explain the goals of Project Citizen and evaluate how each of the five concepts discussed in this section shape civic engagement in the community.

Suggested 5E Inquiry Lesson Plan

Engage

Engage your students by taking the following steps:

1. Start a group discussion: say, "What is a community? Think about where you live and who you interact with."
2. Say, "What are some types of communities you belong to?" Provide suggestions, such as school, sports teams, religious groups, and online communities.
3. Say, "How do these communities affect your life?" Ask students to think about how each community shapes their experiences, values, and how they interact with others.
4. Record responses on the board or on a shared digital platform, such as a Google Doc.
5. Share the compelling question for Chapter 1: "Do I have the power to create change in my community?" Ask students to read silently or in trio teams/small groups the purpose of Chapter 1. Ask the follow-up question: "What do you think is the main idea or purpose of Chapter 1, based on what you read?"
6. Share the first supporting question: "Who are the citizens in Project Citizen?" Ask students to connect this question back to the discussion of their different types of communities.
7. In small groups or as a whole class, have students read this section.
8. Ask students, based on what they have read, how they would answer the question. Say, "The passage talks about two ways of understanding citizenship, one that is based on a legal status and another that focuses on being an active member of the community. Why do you think it is important to recognize the broader definition of citizenship?"
9. Share the next supporting question: "Do I have a role in the American political system?" Ask students to connect this question back to the discussion of their different types of communities. Be sure to record student responses on a board or a shared digital document.
10. In small groups or as a whole class, have students read the section: "Do I Have a Role in the American Political System?"
11. Ask students, based on what they have read, how they would answer the question: "What are various ways citizens can contribute to and participate in their communities?"

Teaching Suggestions

- You may want to explain to students that resolving problems within public policy is the only way governmental action can change.
- These first two supporting questions in Chapter 1 are important for students to understand the program and to be able to see themselves in it. Teachers should spend appropriate time setting the context and addressing students' questions about their role in the community and in Project Citizen.
- Use the Do You Know? questions to help students make connections to prior knowledge. Consider deepening student connections by sharing the Gettysburg Address or the text from the Pledge of Allegiance.

Explore

1. Share the next supporting question: What are the foundations of the American government?

2. Have students look at the initial list of principles in this section. Without reading their descriptions yet, ask the class what principles they recognize and believe are most foundational to the American political system. Record their answers on the board or a shared document for reference.

3. Divide the class into groups of five. Assign each student in the group to read the text about one of the five foundational principles from the first chapter of the student edition and become an expert on classical republicanism, classical liberalism, federalism, popular sovereignty, and representative government. See the Understanding Foundational Principles graphic organizer in the appendix of this teacher's guide.

4. Each student reads their assigned principle, focusing on understanding the main ideas and key points.

5. After reading, students share with their group members what their assigned principle was about, with main ideas and key points, and answer any questions group members may have.

6. Ask students to reflect on the principles. Discuss in small groups whether they see similarities and differences in the principles. Say, "Do you notice any similarities or differences between the five principles? Discuss any differences and similarities you may see with the foundational principles and record those on your charts."

7. Have students complete the reflection question: Something I found surprising about foundational principles was …

8. In small groups or as a whole class, have students read the section: "What Are the Foundations of the American Government?"

Explain

1. Explain to students that they will be reflecting on the communities they belong to and how these communities influence them.

2. Remind students that communities can include various groups of people and organizations that students belong to and interact with.

3. Ensure each student has a copy of the Graphic Organizer: Community Mapping from the student edition. Note that, as with all handouts associated with this text, a digital version of this organizer can be printed or shared with students so they can fill in information via their own document. URLs to the handouts can be found below the resource in the student edition.

4. Instruct students to write their name at the center of the graphic organizer.

5. Encourage students to brainstorm and list all the communities they belong to.

6. Students should write the names of these communities inside each surrounding circle (one community name per circle).

7. Have students write unique characteristics of each community inside its respective circle.
   A. Does that community have a shared identity or identities?
   B. Does that community have a unifying activity, such as a performance, competition, or group meetings?
   C. Is it part of or connected to an even larger community?

8. Students draw lines from the center circle to each community circle to show how the communities are connected to them.

9. Facilitate small-group discussions where students can share their completed form with their group.
   A. Are there any similarities among the communities?
   B. Are there any differences among the communities?
   C. Are there communities that have a greater impact than others?

Elaborate

1. Introduce the Collaborate Together: Understanding Foundational Principles activity to students, explaining they will be working in trio teams/small groups to develop answers to questions about what they have learned so far.
2. Discuss the expectations of participation in the activity, such as active engagement, respectful communication, and collaboration.
3. Divide the class into trio teams/small groups. Consider factors such as student strengths and student dynamics when forming groups.
4. Ensure that each question is clearly presented and accessible to all group members.
   A. Give examples from the American political system of each of the five concepts—classical republicanism, classical liberalism, federalism, popular sovereignty, and representative government—that they have studied. This can be added to the Understanding Foundational Principles graphic organizer in the appendix of this teacher's guide.
   B. What other terms or concepts might you use to describe the American political system (i.e., democracy, rule of law, etc.)?
   C. What is the difference between a right and a responsibility? Give examples of each of these.
   D. What is civic virtue? Do you believe most Americans practice civic virtue when participating in public life? Why or why not?
   E. What is enlightened self-interest? How is enlightened self-interest connected to civic virtue? How are they different?
   F. What are some real-life examples where individual rights and the common good might conflict with each other?
   G. Why was it important for the U.S. Constitution to divide powers between the national and state governments?
5. Circulate around the classroom to provide guidance and clarification as needed.
6. Instruct the groups to be prepared to present and discuss their answers with the entire class once they have completed their discussions.
7. Facilitate a whole-class discussion where each group presents their answers to the questions discussed.

Teaching Suggestions

If you have time constraints during the whole-class discussion, consider having one group share their answers for each question.

Evaluate

1. Reintroduce the compelling question, "Do I have the power to create change in my community?" Have students discuss why or why not in trio teams/small groups.

2. Introduce What Do You Think? Roles for Participation in Democracy to students. Explain that they will be individually answering questions related to citizenship and democracy and answering questions about their opinions and responsibilities as citizens.

3. Emphasize to students that it is okay if they are not confident in all of their answers at this stage. The purpose of the activity is to set a baseline for knowledge and beliefs about one's role in a democracy.

4. Ensure each student has a copy of the What Do You Think? exercise. Ask students to read each question carefully and provide thoughtful responses based on their understanding of citizenship and democracy.

5. Encourage students to continue thinking about these questions and concepts as they progress through the project. Let them know they will answer these exact same questions once they have completed Project Citizen, and they will likely see some change or growth in their reflections.

6. Have students discuss the compelling question, "Do I have the power to create change in my community?"

7. As an exit ticket, have students answer the compelling question.

Teaching Suggestions

These responses should be kept until the end of the project so that students can compare their answers before and after completing Project Citizen. This may be used as a pre- and post-test to demonstrate student growth and the development of civic dispositions. One way to collect and keep these initial student responses is to create a shared digital folder for students to save their responses to in order to view them at the end of the project. Another option would be to copy and print the organizer, have students complete it by hand, and collect and file responses in order to distribute once students complete the final form at the end of the project.

Media Literacy Moments

Purpose

The Media Literacy Moment activities throughout the student edition play a pivotal role in guiding students to understand the significance of media literacy within Project Citizen. Through a structured approach, students are introduced to fundamental concepts of media literacy through introductory paragraphs. These serve as a springboard for interactive activities designed to deepen students' comprehension and critical-thinking skills regarding media consumption and creation.

Throughout this teacher's guide, there are suggestions to support educators in effectively integrating media literacy into the curriculum. These resources offer valuable insights and strategies for accommodating diverse learning styles and enhancing media-literacy instruction.

Media Literacy Moment

Find It on **Page 9** of the Student Edition

Does a Free Press Support Democracy?

1. Pose the media-literacy question, "Does a free press support democracy?"
2. Encourage students to share their answers with the class.
3. In small groups or as a whole class, have students read the question from the media literacy moment, "Does a free press support democracy?"
4. Divide the class into trio teams/small groups. Ensure that each group has a designated space in the classroom to work collaboratively.
5. Instruct each group to brainstorm as many ways as they can think of in which a free press supports democracy.
6. Provide each group with a large sheet of paper or poster board to record their answers on. Remind students to write legibly so others can easily read their answers.
7. Have students hang up their posters around the classroom.
8. Students will participate in a gallery walk where they move around the classroom to visit each poster and consider their classmates' responses. Remind students to pay attention to any new ideas that they see.
9. Once they have completed the gallery walk, have them return to their groups and discuss any new ideas they saw on other posters. Students can add new ideas to their own posters.
10. Students will independently reflect on the role a free press plays in supporting democracy by completing a written reflection. Provide students with the following prompts.
    A. What is a free press?
    B. How does a free press contribute to informing citizens about issues relevant to democracy?
    C. In what ways does a free press help hold government officials and institutions accountable?
    D. How does access to diverse news sources and perspectives enhance democratic participation and decision making?
11. Facilitate a whole-class discussion where students can share their reflections. Encourage them to consider ideas shared during the gallery walk and group discussions.

Continued on the Next Page →

← Continued From the Previous Page

Teaching Suggestions

- Music during gallery walk: Consider playing music softly in the background during the gallery walk to signal when students should move to the next poster.
- Audio or video recording for reflections: Offer students the option to complete their journal reflections as audio or video recordings. Some students may find it more comfortable to express their thoughts verbally rather than in written form.
- Group-formation considerations: When creating groups, consider students' strengths, interests, and working styles to ensure effective collaboration. Aim for balanced groups that include a mix of abilities and personalities.
- Virtual considerations: Conduct the gallery walk virtually by using digital-collaboration tools or shared digital-presentation tools. Each group can create a slide or space to display their brainstormed ideas, and students can rotate through the virtual gallery to view and comment on each other's answers. Use breakout rooms on Zoom or Microsoft Teams to facilitate small-group discussions and brainstorming sessions. Assign students to breakout rooms based on their group. Be sure to provide clear instructions for collaboration and recording of ideas. Allow students to complete their written reflections digitally using word-processing software, online-journal platforms, or voice-recording apps. Alternatively, students can record audio or video reflections using video-conferencing tools.

2

Do We Need Public Policy?

Purpose

This chapter provides background information that is useful in understanding the meaning of the term *public policy* and the role of public policy in local, state, and national government. When students have completed this lesson, they should be able to identify the private sphere, civil society, and government as the three parts of society. Students should also be able to evaluate, take, and defend positions on which parts of society may be best suited to deal with certain problems. Finally, students should be able to explain the role of public policy in dealing with common problems of society.

This lesson contains material about topics encouraging students to make decisions based on their own individual values. Of course, answers will vary among students. This material has been included to provide students with a sense of the role our personal values play in societal decisions. A culturally responsive classroom will provide a welcoming and safe environment where students feel comfortable discussing difficult topics. Ensure students feel comfortable sharing appropriate personal perspectives. Consider establishing classroom norms that encourage discussion.

Suggested 5E Inquiry Lesson Plan

Engage

1. Share the Chapter 2 question with students: "Do we need public policy?"
2. Share with students that they will be "voting with their feet" by moving to different parts of the room according to their views on whether each issue should be a public or private matter. This activity helps students understand the role of public policy in addressing social issues and whether public intervention is necessary or whether matters can be effectively managed privately.
3. Write the words *Private* and *Public* on different sides of the board at the front of the classroom or on different sides of the classroom.
4. Read an issue and tell students to stand, based on their answer to the question, on either the "private" or "public" side ("voting with their feet"). Tell students to consider whether the issue should be handled privately—within the home, by individuals, or private organizations; or publicly—requiring intervention or regulation by a government or public entity.

Teaching Suggestions

You may want to provide further context here. For a private matter, think about whether individuals or families can manage this issue on their own, without needing government intervention. For a public matter, consider whether the issue requires laws, regulations, or support from the government or public institutions to be effectively addressed.

5. Ask students to explain why they think the issue is a private or public matter with the others on their side of the classroom.
6. Read the next issue and let students decide again. Emphasize differing opinions.

7. This activity should not be viewed as a competitive debate but as an example of the spectrum of views on the role of government.
8. In trio teams/small groups, discuss the following questions:
   A. Can private solutions effectively address all the issues we discussed? Why or why not?
   B. Based on our discussion, do you think we need public policy? Why or why not?
   C. Should either the government or individuals decide the following situations?
      ▷ The appropriate limitations on social media used to prevent the spread of misinformation
      ▷ Companies tracking an individual's online activity in order to target advertising
      ▷ Adults vaping in public places
      ▷ The amount of soda a person can buy at fast-food restaurants
      ▷ Requiring people to wear seatbelts

Teaching Suggestions

Emphasize that practically all Americans agree that we need government to regulate some things. The debate is around what topics government should get involved with and to what degree.

9. Share the compelling question for Chapter 2 again: "Do we need public policy?"
10. Ask students to read silently or in pairs the purpose of Chapter 2.
11. Have students answer in trio teams/small groups the compelling question, "Do we need public policy?"

Explore

1. Share supporting question 1: "What are the private sphere, civil society, and government?"

2. Ask students to connect this question back to their discussion of topics that should be considered public or private. What sphere would they guess each topic belongs to?

3. In small groups or as a whole class, have students read this section. Discuss and clarify after students complete their reading.

4. Students work individually or in trio teams/ small groups to complete Making Connections: Distinguishing Among Spheres Society in the student edition.

Answers

| 1. C | 2. B | 3. A | 4. A | 5. B |
| 6. D | 7. C | 8. B | 9. D | 10. C |

5. Have students share their answers in trio teams/ small groups.

6. Lead a whole-class discussion to ensure students understand the roles of each sphere.

7. Share supporting question 2: "Which Areas of Society Should Deal with Certain Problems?"

8. In small groups or as a whole class, have students read this section. Discuss and clarify after students complete their reading.

9. Ask students to think about the types of problems that might cause people to have different opinions about the three different spheres of society—government, civil, and private—that should be responsible for dealing with them.

10. Have students give examples of these types of problems, such as affordable housing, environmental protection, gun ownership, healthcare, drug and alcohol use, and homelessness. Note: This is a good opportunity for discussion of comparative government— people in other countries have very different ideas about the role of government.

For example, in most European countries, healthcare is widely expected to be a service the government must provide for all citizens, whereas in the United States, we have a largely private healthcare system.

11. Students work in trio teams/small groups to complete the Collaborate Together: Whose Responsibility Is It? activity in the student edition. We recommend students do the Collaborate Together: Whose Responsibility Is It? as the Explore activity, even though it comes after the public policy reading, because it lends itself to student exploration.

12. Explain to students that they will be examining common societal problems and determining what part of society should primarily be responsible for addressing each problem.

13. Instruct students to read through each problem listed on the activity in groups and determine whether the problem should be primarily addressed by private, civil, or governmental spheres.

14. Encourage students to use the sentence starters provided in the activity to help them define their answers.
    - **Private sphere:** I think people in our community should help solve this because ...
    - **Civil society:** Groups like clubs and charities could make a difference by ...
    - **Government:** The government needs to do something about this issue because ...

15. Circulate around the classroom to monitor student progress, provide clarification, or answer questions.

16. Have groups share their answers with the whole group.

Answers

| 1. A | 2. C | 3. B | 4. A | 5. C |
| 6. C | 7. B | 8. C | 9. C | 10. C |

Teaching Suggestions for Collaborate Together: Whose Responsibility Is It?

- Students work individually or in small groups to complete the Collaborate Together: Whose Responsibility Is It? activity in the student edition. Some students may find a graphic organizer useful for this activity. They could write each problem under one heading or in a box labeled "private sphere," "civil society," or "government." Differences among students in their responses to these questions should be respected.
- Students could also complete this exercise by walking around the room to different areas labeled with the three spheres. Have them complete a debrief on whether they see any patterns. For instance, some students may tend to think the private sphere should deal with most things related to childcare, but that the government should take care of building bridges, roads, and other infrastructure, while others feel the government should provide paid family leave and free early-childhood education.
- Student responses should be evaluated on the basis of the reasoning and evidence they give to support their positions.

Explain

Tell students that while working on Project Citizen, they will focus on problems for which the government could be responsible. These are issues that are in the "public" rather than "private" domain. The government develops "policies"—laws, rules, regulations, orders, plans, or actions—to deal with these problems. Therefore, we will use the phrase "public policy" to refer to government's responses to these types of problems.

1. Share supporting question 3: "What is Public Policy?"

2. Utilize the "Know, Wonder, Learn" (KWL) chart found in the appendix or display one on the board or in a shared digital document.

3. Ask students to brainstorm different types of policies they are familiar with in their daily lives. Provide examples, such as school rules (graduation requirements, dress code, tardy policies, etc.) and traffic regulations (speed limits, parking violations, etc.). Have students add this under the K on the KWL graphic organizer for "Know." This KWL chart can be found in Appendix A.

4. As a class, discuss what students would like to learn about public policy. Add their responses to the KWL chart. Policies that students know go under the Know column. List policies or concepts that students have questions about under the Wonder column. Have students add this under the W on the KWL graphic organizer for "Wonder."

5. In trio teams/small groups, have students read the text section under supporting question 3: "What is public policy?" Tell groups to pause periodically to discuss the following:
   A. The definition of public policy, after students finish reading.
   B. Implementation of public policies. Discuss and clarify the four alternative ways public policy might be implemented.
   C. Procedural justice and the development and implementation of public policy. Discuss and clarify the meaning of the term *procedural justice*—or due process of law—and its goals, as well as the considerations to take into account in determining whether procedures used by the government are fair.

6. After discussing in trio teams/small groups, have the whole class discuss what they have learned about public policy. After the discussion, have groups share out to the whole class. Complete the Learn section of the KWL chart.

7. Describe the purpose of the activity Collaborate Together: Problem Solvers, which is to analyze scenarios and determine how public policy is applied to each situation.

8. Provide an example for students, such as civil society solving problems alone (e.g., a group of volunteers organizing a fundraising event to support a local animal shelter).

9. Model your thinking process by discussing how you would analyze a scenario and determine which description best fits. Explain your reasoning.

10. Divide the class into trio teams/small groups.

11. Instruct students to carefully read each scenario and determine which description (A, B, C, or D) best fits the situation.

12. Encourage students to discuss their reasoning within their groups and be prepared to explain their choices for a class discussion.

13. Students work individually or in small groups to complete Collaborate Together: Problem Solvers in the student edition.

Answers
1. A 2. B 3. D 4. A 5. D
6. B 7. B 8. D 9. B 10. A

14. Reconvene as a whole class and facilitate a discussion where groups share their answers for each scenario, once groups have completed the activity.

Teaching Suggestions

- Post the KWL chart throughout the Project Citizen process. Encourage students to add to each section of the chart as they have more questions.
- Teachers may also find it useful to have students complete the Graphic Organizer: Policy Doctor–Making the Right Diagnosis (see the "Elaborate" section below) first in small groups, and then have them complete the activity Collaborate Together: Problem Solvers as a form of quiz to assess individual student learning.

Elaborate

1. Introduce the Graphic Organizer: Policy Doctor—Making the Right Diagnosis activity.
2. Divide the class into trio teams/small groups.
3. Instruct students to read each scenario carefully and discuss which sphere of society—government, civil, or private—is responsible for addressing the problem.
4. After determining each sphere, instruct students to determine who is in charge of making the rules of policies to address the problem.
5. Guide students through the example scenario. Discuss the issue presented (students believe the dress code does not apply to all students equally) and identify the responsible sphere (government) and potential decision makers (school board, administrators, etc.).
6. After completing the activity, facilitate a whole-class discussion. Have groups share their analyses for each scenario and discuss any differences in perspectives.
7. Now that students better understand which spheres of society are responsible for different issues, they are going to dive deeper into what specific issues are considered public policy problems. This will help with identifying and selecting problems for their project.
8. Share supporting question 4: "What kinds of issues are public policy problems?"
9. In small groups or as a whole class, have students read the section, "What Kinds of Issues are Public Policy Problems?"
10. Discuss and clarify the reasons for Project Citizen's focus on public policy problems.
11. Divide students into trio teams/small groups as they answer the Stop and Reflect question: "In what ways can individuals and communities advocate for changes in public policy to address community challenges?"
12. Facilitate a whole-class discussion where groups share their suggestions for ways individuals and communities can advocate for changes in public policy.
13. As groups share their ideas, record each suggestion on a digital document or board for all students to see.
14. Have students explain the reasonings behind their suggestions. Once all groups have shared their ideas, be sure the recorded list of suggestions is accessible to students for future reference.

Evaluate

1. To evaluate learning, students will complete the Graphic Organizer: Creating Solutions activity in the student project guide.
2. Working in trio teams/small groups, students will analyze community problems and brainstorm potential public policy and civil-society solutions.
3. Instruct students to read the first example of a community problem provided in the middle column. Then, guide students to examine the examples of public policy solutions by the government (column one) and solutions owned by civil society (column three) for the given problem.
4. Direct students to complete the chart with their own suggestions for public policy and civil-society solutions to the remaining problems listed.
5. Be sure students understand to use the blank column to identify a problem in their own community and provide examples of potential public policy and civil-society solutions to address it.

Teaching Suggestions

- Teachers may consider modeling the first item on the chart as an example to ensure students understand expectations. Say, "The community problem is the lack of access to nutritious food. What are some public policy solutions?"
- As students are providing public policy solutions, use the answers on the chart for the public policy solutions to guide their answers. Repeat with civil-society solutions.
- The completed graphic organizer below shows some sample responses.

Public Policy Solution	Community Problems	Civil-Society Solution
City officials fund a program to give families who are experiencing food insecurity a credit to buy food from participating merchants.	Lack of access to nutritious food	Members of a local temple conduct a drive to collect food for families experiencing food insecurity.
Local government implements rent-control measures to limit the amount landlords can increase rent.	Lack of affordable housing.	Nonprofit organizations partner with local businesses to build affordable housing.
Government implements stricter laws and regulations on cyberbullying.	Online harassment affecting a growing number of students	Community organizations and schools organize workshops and seminars on digital citizenship to teach students how to protect themselves and others from online harassment.
Local government adds bike lanes and crosswalks and implements stricter traffic laws for pedestrian and cyclist safety.	Increased car accidents involving pedestrians and cyclists.	Advocacy groups and neighborhood associations organize community campaigns to raise awareness about pedestrian and cyclist safety.
Local government allocates funding to create and maintain public parks and playgrounds in residential areas.	A lack of safe places to play outside for neighborhood children.	Community members and local businesses collaborate to establish a neighborhood-watch program.
School guidance counselors set up afterschool support groups to support student mental health.	High school students struggling with mental health issues.	Mental-health advocacy groups organize peer support groups for students.

Evaluate (continued)

6. To more formally check for understanding, have students complete Exit Ticket: Triangle, Square, Circle, which can be found in the appendix.

7. On their exit tickets, students should write three points they learned about public policy today next to the triangle. They will write something that squares with them (i.e., makes sense and seems important) about answering the inquiry question: "Do we need public policy?" next to the square. Students then write a question that is still circling with them about public policy, such as, "Which sphere is responsible for addressing an issue?," "Is there a difference in the three spheres?," or "What kinds of issues are public policy?"

Extension Activity

The range of reasonable views on issues in both the public and private spheres provides an opportunity to teach students about different political parties and political views. Students may conduct online research to learn about the philosophies of the major political parties and how each party differs in its views about issues in the public and private spheres. An enlightening contrast is provided by the Libertarian and Green Party platforms, as well as the platforms of the Republican and Democratic parties. Students could complete a graphic organizer and discuss their findings in class.

3 How Does Project Citizen Empower My Engagement in Public Policy?

Purpose

In this chapter, your students will conduct an investigation into problems facing their community. They will be focusing on problems that most likely require some degree of government action in order for there to be a successful resolution. Students will follow a six-step process that will enable them to identify and study one significant problem, recommend a solution in the form of a public policy proposal, and present their research and proposal in the form of a portfolio and public hearing.

Importantly, the steps within Chapter 3 broadly correlate with the 5Es outlined in the overview of this guide. As a continuation of the 5E Instructional Model used throughout the suggested lessons in this guide, the 5Es naturally support authentic inquiry as students work through each step to develop their project.

Because of the student-led nature of the Project Citizen process, teachers will need ample flexibility to adjust lessons and working time for student research, small-group discussion, and community interviews. For that reason, the format for Chapter 3 is different from the suggested 5E lesson plans accompanying Chapters 1, 2, and 4. Instead, each of the six steps of the Project Citizen process in Chapter 3 will be accompanied by suggestions for teacher moves for every student activity in that step. Each of the six steps in the Project Citizen Process will include a launching activity and an assessment exercise to support teachers in opening and closing each step.

To accentuate how the 5Es exist within this chapter, however, please see the chart on the following page.

Project Citizen Steps and the 5Es

Step	5E Inquiry Alignment
Step 1: Identifying Problems to Be Dealt With by Public Policy	**Engage:** Pique students' interest and get them personally involved in the project by accessing prior knowledge, experiences, and authentic interest in problems in their community.
Step 2: Selecting a Problem or Problems for Your Class to Study	**Explore:** Students begin discovering answers to initial questions about community problems, explore key concepts, probe their own experiences and the experiences of others, and eventually focus their examination on one community issue.
Step 3: Gathering Information on the Problem You Will Study	**Explain:** Use questioning strategies to lead student-led research, connecting their prior knowledge with new information and prompting them to record and communicate their discoveries.
Step 4: Developing a Portfolio to Present Your Research	**Elaborate:** Students solidify their thinking about their topic and select and apply public policy to a real-world presentation of their findings. Students communicate new understandings with formal and academic language that is both authentic and persuasive.
Step 5: Presenting Your Portfolio in a Simulated Public Hearing **Step 6:** Reflecting on Your Experience	**Evaluate:** Students culminate their project experience by demonstrating their understanding of their topic and public policy by presenting their portfolio publicly for evaluation and feedback. Students also reflect on their learning throughout the project process.

1 Identifying Problems to Be Dealt With by Public Policy

Introductory Note

Before diving into public policy, it is essential for students to embark on a journey of self-discovery and community exploration. In this initial step, students are encouraged to reflect on their own values and beliefs, laying the foundation for understanding the issues that resonate most deeply with them. By examining the world through the lens of their personal experiences and perspectives, students can begin to identify pressing problems within their communities that demand attention. Through thoughtful reflection and inquiry, students will gain insight into the diverse array of issues affecting their neighborhoods, schools, and beyond, setting the stage for meaningful engagement in the public policy process.

To help educators implement this step and all subsequent steps, this guide provides an introductory note, purpose, and suggested teacher moves correlated with the activities, reflections, and resources students will be interacting with in each step.

Purpose

In this step, students will identify a number of problems in their community or state that they think should be dealt with primarily by government or by government and civil society acting cooperatively. These can be problems that students may have experienced, or they could be problems that students have heard discussed by others, read about in the news, or learned about from television or social media.

Students will also learn something about each of the problems they have identified and which governmental agencies at the local, state, or national levels are responsible for dealing with the problems.

The purpose of this lesson is to prepare students for Step 2, when the class or groups select a problem to investigate further and propose a public policy solution to the problem as part of their participation in Project Citizen.

Suggested Teacher Moves

Each of the section headers below correspond to the sections, activities, and resources found in Step 1.

Launching Step 1: Identifying Problems to Be Dealt With by Public Policy

1. Ask students, "If you were president for a day and could solve one problem in your community, what problem would you attempt to solve? Why?"
2. Lead a discussion of student responses to the question.
3. Start a list of problems on the board or in a shared digital document. Challenge students to connect and defend their problems as public policy problems, based on the definition of public policy from Chapter 2 of the student edition.
4. Students read the "Purpose" section for Chapter 3 in the student edition. Discuss the purpose and the activities with students.

Explore Together: Identifying Values

1. Discuss the student's role in Project Citizen.
2. Pose the following question: "What role do different levels of government play in addressing community problems?"
3. Lead a class discussion where students share their thoughts and ideas about the roles of government in addressing community problems. Encourage students to think about the division of responsibilities among different levels of government and how this impacts the effectiveness of addressing community problems.
4. Explain to students the importance of understanding their values in identifying issues that matter most to them and their communities.
5. Discuss that values are individual beliefs that guide actions and behaviors, and exploring them can provide insight into personal priorities and community concerns.

Making Connections: Mapping Your Values

1. Distribute the pre-cut value cards to students and explain the categories that students will be sorting the cards into the following categories: Always Valued, Often Valued, Sometimes Valued, Seldom Valued, and Least Valued.
2. Instruct students to sort each value card into the appropriate category based on its significance to them and the way they view the world.
3. Encourage students to think about why each value is important or not important to them as they sort their cards.
4. After sorting their values, have students choose their top-three values and explain why these values are most significant to them.
5. Facilitate group discussions where students compare their values with their classmates' values and identify similarities or differences.
6. Prompt students to consider shared values within their community and discuss the importance of collective values in addressing community issues.
7. Label four corners of the room with the following categories: "Protecting the rights of individuals to life, liberty, and property," "Promoting the common good," "Promoting justice or fairness, including equal opportunities for all people," and "Providing safety and security."
8. Instruct students to move to the corner of the room that best matches their top value card.
9. Once students are in their respective corners, have each corner group discuss why they chose that corner and how their selected values align with the corner's description.

10. Encourage students to make connections with classmates who share similar values and discuss the implications for choosing a problem to focus on for their project.

11. Pose reflection questions to students, such as "How do you think your community's current policies help or hinder the category you chose?" or "What changes and improvements would you propose to better address the chosen topic in your community?"

Graphic Organizer: What Is Bothering You?

1. Explain the importance of understanding community issues and the valuable perspective students can offer in identifying and addressing them.

2. Ensure each student has a copy of the Graphic Organizer: What Is Bothering You? to students and explain the purpose of the activity. Note that this can be downloaded from the URL at the bottom of page 43 in the student edition.

3. Encourage students to identify someone they trust to interview about a community issue that concerns them, and set up the interview using the provided scripts.

4. Explain to students that it is important to actively listen during the interview and ask follow-up questions to better understand the issue.

5. Have students conduct the interview, recording the interviewee's responses in "Section 1: Community-Member Interview" of the graphic organizer.

6. Instruct students to research additional information about the problem named by the interviewee and record their findings in "Section 2: Exploring the Issue."
   ○ Students should consider who deals with the problem, the current policies in place to address the problem, and whether these policies need to be replaced, supplemented, or revised. Students need to think critically about which level or branch of government is responsible for addressing the problem, explaining their reasoning. Students also need to consider the role of government, civil society, and the private sphere in addressing the identified issue and proposing potential solutions.

7. Pose reflection questions to students, such as the following:
   ○ Does the problem identified by the interviewee align with the value you chose? Why or why not?
   ○ How do your personal values influence your perspective on community issues and potential solutions?

Teaching Suggestions

Have students identify a caregiver or family member who can act as a civic-project partner during their exploration of community needs and throughout the Project Citizen process. This adult civic-project partner can provide valuable feedback and guidance to students. Teachers can facilitate this process by

- discussing with students the importance of seeking feedback from someone familiar with the community's needs in the Graphic Organizer: What Is Bothering You?;
- providing guidance on selecting a caregiver or adult who can offer meaningful insights and support throughout the civic project;
- providing guidance to civic-project partners on how to actively participate in discussions, give insights, help students brainstorm ideas, and provide support to students on how to navigate challenges;
- encouraging students to celebrate successes with their selected adult civic-project partner; and
- providing opportunities to students to publicly acknowledge and express gratitude to selected adult civic-project partners throughout the Project Citizen process.

Graphic Organizer: Learning More About the Problems the Class Has Identified

1. Direct the students' attention to the graphic organizer titled "Learning More About the Problems the Class has Identified."

2. Divide the class into small groups of four to six students each.

3. Be sure each group has a designated space to collaborate and discuss.

4. Instruct each group to discuss the community problem they identified through previous activities.

5. On a sheet of paper, have students list all the issues discovered by their group.

6. Assign one student in each group to read the problems aloud to their group. The other group members indicate their level of concern for each problem by holding up a fist to five fingers: fist = I do not care about this problem at all, five fingers = I really care about this problem a lot, etc.

7. Encourage group members to discuss their ratings and reasons for choosing them. If necessary, prompt students by asking the following questions:
   - Why do you think the selected community issue received the highest rating?
   - Were there specific aspects of the issue that resonated with the group or seemed particularly pressing?
   - Did the urgency or impact of the issue contribute to its high rating?

8. Students should count the number of fingers each problem received, then record the total rating for each problem.

9. Students should then choose the community issue with the highest total rating as the focus for the rest of the project. Have one student from each group present the group's collective decision to the class, explaining the reasoning behind their choice. Consider debriefing the activity by asking the following questions:
   - What factors did you and your group consider when rating each community issue?
   - How did personal experiences, community concerns, or other considerations influence your ratings?
   - How did group discussions and consensus building contribute to the final ratings?

Rating Problems and Narrowing in on Root Causes

1. Direct the students' attention to the subsection of the graphic organizer on page 47 of the student edition titled "Rating Problems and Narrowing In on Root Causes."

2. Instruct students to review the list of community issues each group created and the ratings each issue was given for each, reflecting on how they arrived at their final ratings, as well as the factors that influenced their decision-making process.
   - There are sentence stems in the student edition to support student discourse and discussion. Encourage students to use the provided sentence stems to articulate their thoughts and reasoning clearly. These stems can support students in expressing their ideas and insights effectively.

3. To help students understand the process of identifying root causes, use the following example:
   - Problem: My neighbor was in a bad car accident at a local intersection.
     - Why? His car was hit by a truck.
     - Why? Because the truck did not have to stop at the intersection.

- ▷ Why? Because there is no stop sign or stoplight.
- ▷ Why? Because the intersection is part of a busy truck stop.
- ▷ Why? Because there is no off-ramp from the highway to the truck stop.

4. Guide students to apply the "Five Whys" technique to their highest-rated community issue. Encourage them to record their answers and identify the nearest root cause for each why. This process will help students delve deeper into understanding the underlying factors contributing to the identified problem.

Extension Activity

1. Review what public policy is and how it affects communities.
2. You may want to show examples of public policy issues, such as broken sidewalks or lack of pedestrian crossings.
3. Explain that, for this assignment, students will take photos of issues in their neighborhood and bring them back for discussion.
4. Ask students to walk around their neighborhood and identify areas that could benefit from public policy changes. Examples include safety concerns (missing stop signs, dangerous crosswalks), infrastructure needs (potholes, broken streetlights), and environmental concerns (littering, lack of recycling bins).
5. Instruct students to take clear photos of the issues they identify. Encourage them to take photos from multiple angles, if necessary. Students then write a brief description of each issue they photograph, including the location of the issue, why they think it is a problem, and possible solutions they envision.
6. Display the submitted photos to the class or have students present them. Ask questions that drive their discovery of the issues.
   - ○ What is the issue shown?
   - ○ Why is it important to address?
   - ○ What are some possible solutions?
   - ○ How can the community or local government be involved in solving this issue?

2 Selecting a Problem or Problems for Your Class to Study

Introductory Note

In this step, students will select a problem to study that will become the central focus of their Project Citizen experience from this point forward.

This is a very important step for the teacher to monitor to ensure that students select appropriate problems to study. Selecting a problem may be a quick and easy process with some classes if the students have already become interested in a small number of problems during the previous steps and can reach consensus on one problem without extensive debate. In other classes, this may be one of the more time-consuming steps of Project Citizen because students debate and discuss the merits of selecting from among a wide range of problems they are interested in. The teacher must guide the class through this step by providing the level of structure the students need in their particular circumstances.

Finally, the teacher must exercise an appropriate level of control over the problems students are allowed to select. Teachers maintain veto power over student-selected problems, if necessary, to ensure that students research problems the teacher and the community deem appropriate for them to study in great depth. Furthermore, teachers may choose to direct students toward problems at the level of government—federal, state, local, or school—they want students to learn most about, depending on the goal they want to accomplish with the Project Citizen project. Teachers could allow students a great deal of freedom in selecting problems by allowing them to research any problems that interest them. It is important to note that research has shown students are more motivated and learn more when they are allowed to choose the problem they work on.

Purpose

In this step, the entire class will discuss the problems the individual groups researched. When there is enough information to select a single problem for further study, the students will be asked to conduct in-depth research into the issue. By the end of this step, students should have selected a problem that they will focus on for the remainder of the Project Citizen experience.

Suggested Teacher Moves

Each of the section headers below correspond to the sections, activities, and resources found in Step 2.

Launching Step 2: Selecting a Problem or Problems for Your Class to Study

1. Ask students to think about which issue they want to select as a class problem for Project Citizen. If the class has already compiled a list, give them time to review the collected problems.

2. Have each student write a brief statement that answers the following questions:
   - What problem do you want your group to study for Project Citizen?
   - Why do you think this problem is the most important and appropriate problem for the class to study for the next few weeks?

3. Collect and share each student's suggested problem with the class. This can be done by students reading their statement out loud to the class. Students can share in trio teams/small groups, or the teacher can collect statements from the class and share.

Sharing Information on Community Problems and Recommending a Problem to Study

1. Students read the "Purpose" section for Step 2 in the student edition.

2. Discuss the purpose with the class. Clarify that students will be able to form small groups based on the problems they are interested in studying. The entire class will ideally study the same problem unless you have decided that each group should study its own problem. Emphasize that today is the day to make a final decision about what problem they will study for the rest of Project Citizen.

Selecting a Problem to Study

1. Compile a list of potential topics for the public policy project based on student suggestions from the earlier launching steps. Teachers could also have students compile a list in groups.

2. Determine how the topics will be displayed for voting, whether through physical posters, a whiteboard, or a digital platform.

3. Have students share their responses in trio teams/small groups. Each group member should make a recommendation for or against taking on the problem. Groups could form around broad topics like education, health, environment, crime, transportation, etc. The groups will then decide on a problem based on their discussion.

4. Have each group share with the rest of the class the problem their group chose. Record the list on the board or a shared digital document. Be sure it is a problem that
   - should be addressed or resolved by government acting alone or by government acting in cooperation with civil society or the private sphere,
   - is important to students and their communities,
   - students can gather enough information about to develop a good project, and
   - students might actually be able to address or resolve by proposing a public policy to officials of their community, state, or federal government.

Collaborate Together: Pick the Problem

1. Post the list of potential topics in a visible location in the classroom or on a digital platform accessible to all students. You may have groups create this list in their groups. Ensure that each topic is clearly written and easy to read.

2. Distribute five sticky notes or similar voting tokens to each student.

3. Instruct students to review the list of topics and select their top choices by placing their sticky notes next to the corresponding topics.

4. Allow students to distribute their votes however they prefer, whether by placing all five votes on one topic or spreading them out among multiple topics.

5. Once all students have cast their votes, collect the sticky notes and tally the votes for each topic.

6. Record the number of votes received for each topic to determine the most popular choices.

7. Discuss the results of the voting process with the class. Encourage students to share their thoughts, preferences, and reasons for voting the way they did.

8. Identify the topics that received the most votes and highlight them as potential candidates for the public policy project.

9. Guide the class in making a collective decision on the priority topic for the public policy project.

Teaching Suggestions

1. For selecting a problem to study, consider using digital platforms for building consensus or voting. Utilize a digital collaboration platform, such as Miro, Padlet, or Google Jamboard, for posting the list of topics and conducting the voting process. This allows students to vote remotely and asynchronously.

2. Digital corkboard: Create a digital corkboard where students can view and interact with the list of topics virtually. Encourage students to use digital sticky notes or markers to vote for their preferred topics directly on the digital platform.

3. Anonymous voting: Consider implementing an anonymous voting process to encourage students to vote based on their genuine preferences, without influence from peers. This can be achieved through digital platforms or by collecting physical votes in a confidential manner.

Extension Activity: The Four Factors

Our public policymakers have limited time, energy, and resources to commit to solving the multitude of problems that people observe. Therefore, policymakers prioritize the problems and implement policies to address only the most pressing problems before them. This realization helps students select problems that are most likely to gain attention from policymakers and to avoid those that are likely to remain low on policymakers' agendas. Students can use the graphic organizer in Appendix A to complete the following activity.

These four factors help determine whether policymakers will focus on a problem. Discuss the importance of policymakers' perceptions of citizens' views of these four factors.

1. **Scope**
   - How widespread is the problem? How many people are affected by it?
     ▷ Problems that affect a large percentage of people are more likely to gain the attention of public policymakers than problems that only affect a fraction of the population.
2. **Intensity**
   - How troublesome is the problem? How concerned are people about the issue? How worked up, passionate, and intense are people about it?
     ▷ Problems that people care deeply about are more likely to gain the attention of public policymakers than problems that people do not care about.

3. **Duration**
   - How long has this been a problem?
     ▷ Consider that the longer an issue attracts the interest of an affected population, the more likely that sizable numbers of that group will demand change from public policymakers.
4. **Resources**
   - What is at stake because of this problem? What might people gain or lose, depending on the response of public policymakers?
     ▷ Resources include financial costs, personal values, ideals, and loyalties that are affected by choosing to address or ignore a particular problem.

To help students understand the importance of the four factors in selecting public policy issues, discuss the questions under each factor in relation to the problems the class is considering. The following activity provides a visual and interactive way to accomplish this. The activity can be carried out using any method of data capture you prefer.

1. Using a scale from 1–5 (lowest to highest), have the entire class rate each problem according to the four factors—scope, intensity, duration, and resources.
2. When all problems have been rated, add up the total points for each one.
3. The problem with the most points is the public policy problem that has enough strength to capture the attention of public policymakers.

After studying the four factors, students may be asked to show that the problem they want to study has high rankings for each factor. This discussion gets students to think about how they can demonstrate that this problem is important enough to go forward with.

3 Gathering Information on the Problem You Will Study

Introductory Note

In Step 3, students dive into the essential task of gathering information from diverse sources to inform their Project Citizen project. They explore various resources, including interviews, articles, and government publications, to gather valuable insights into their chosen community issues. While students may encounter challenges with the interviewing process and setting up interviews, the Project Citizen text offers support and resources to guide them through these obstacles.

Teachers play a pivotal role in modeling effective interviewing techniques and assisting students in navigating the process, ensuring they gain confidence and proficiency in gathering information.

Students also learn the importance of documenting their sources meticulously, laying the foundation for an annotated bibliography that showcases the credibility and depth of their research. As students navigate this step, they acquire essential skills in research and documentation, setting the stage for the development of a compelling portfolio and presentation.

Purpose

Now that the class has selected a problem to study, students must decide where to get additional information. Students already have some information on problems in their community that they gathered in Step 1.

In the activities below, students will collect additional information on the problem or problems the class is studying. Students will employ a variety of resources, including the internet, news sources, printed material, and individuals with special knowledge related to the problem.

Suggested Teacher Moves

Each of the section headers below correspond to the sections, activities, and resources found in Step 3.

Launching Step 3: Gathering Information on the Problem You Will Study

1. Ask students, "How could you find out more about the problem you selected?" Instruct them to list five sources where they could learn more about this problem.

2. Discuss students' answers to the question. Make a list on the board of sources of information as students answer. Ask probing questions to get students to think about specific sources of information. You could say, for example, "Citing the internet as a source is too broad. How—specifically—will you find out more about the problem on the internet? What are specific sites, searches, keywords, and organizations you can use?"

3. Students read the "Purpose" section in the student edition. Discuss the purpose and the activities with students. Emphasize that the main purpose of this step is to gather facts, statistics, articles, and information from experts that will demonstrate that students have selected a serious problem that deserves the attention of policymakers.

The Problem You Will Study

1. Ask students, "How could you find out more about the problem you selected?" Instruct them to list five sources where they could learn more about this problem.

2. Discuss student answers to the question. Make a list of sources of information on the board as students answer. Ask probing questions to get students to think about specific sources of information: "The internet is too broad; how will you find out more about the problem on the internet? Specific sites, searches, keywords, organizations?"

3. Students read the "Purpose" section in the student edition. Discuss the purpose and the activities with students. Emphasize that the main purpose of this step is to gather facts, statistics, articles, and information from experts that will demonstrate that students have selected a serious problem that deserves the attention of policymakers.

Why Is It Important to Gather Information From a Variety of Sources?

1. Students read "A. Why Is It Important to Gather Information from a Variety of Sources?" in the student edition. Ask students, "What are some characteristics of reliable and trustworthy news?" Allow students time to share their responses.

2. Follow up by asking students how the passage discusses civic virtue and the responsibilities of being a citizen. Explain how consuming and creating accurate information is related to being a responsible citizen.

3. Have students discuss in trio teams/small groups and then share with the class.

Identifying Sources of Information

1. Students read "B. Identifying Sources of Information" in the student edition. Discuss the list of sources, adding to the list generated by the class from the initial question. Discuss the strengths and weaknesses of each source relative to the problem the class has selected. Teachers should help students decide what types of research are most likely to yield valuable information about the problem and what sources are realistically available to their students.

Teaching Suggestions

In addition to traditional sources, like internet articles, encourage students to explore personal narratives and interviews as another source of information to provide diverse perspectives on public policy.

2. Begin by reviewing with the students the list of sources of information provided. Discuss the various types of sources and their potential relevance to different types of problems or issues.

3. Guide students to consider the specific problem they are studying for their project and think about which sources of information would be most helpful in addressing that problem.

4. Instruct students to form small groups. Have groups identify and list the sources of information they believe would be most beneficial for their project. They should consider why each source is relevant and how it could contribute to their understanding of the problem.

5. After students have listed their chosen sources, have them share their selections and reasoning with the class. Encourage students to explain why they chose these sources and how they think the sources will assist them in their project.

6. Provide guidance and feedback as needed to ensure students are selecting appropriate and relevant sources for their project.

Guidelines for Obtaining and Documenting Information

1. Divide the class into small research groups or assign research roles to individual students based on the sources of information identified for the project.

2. Explain to students that each research group or role will be responsible for gathering information from two or more sources related to the project.

3. Review the guidelines provided in the student project guide for contacting sources of information. Emphasize the importance of professionalism and clarity in communication when reaching out to offices or individuals.

4. Guide groups to assign specific tasks to group members within each research group or role. For example, designate one student to make phone calls or send emails to offices, while another student may be responsible for scheduling appointments or conducting interviews.

5. Instruct students to document all information obtained from their research activities accurately and thoroughly. Remind them to keep track of correspondence, notes from interviews, and any other relevant materials.

6. Be sure to offer students support with drafting emails, making phone calls, and conducting interviews, as needed.

A Note on Making a Change to the Project

Reinforce the idea that making changes to the project based on research findings is a normal and valuable part of the process. Encourage students to remain flexible and open-minded as they gather information and refine their project focus.

Resource: Introducing Yourself for an Interview

1. Review the provided sample email template and phone-call script with students, emphasizing the importance of professionalism, clarity, and courtesy in communication.
2. Discuss the key components of effective communication, including introducing themselves properly, stating the purpose of the communication, and expressing gratitude for the recipient's time and expertise.
3. Encourage students to personalize the templates and scripts to fit their specific project and target audience. Remind them to include relevant details, such as their school name, grade level, and contact information.

Additional Note on Communicating With Local Leaders

Discuss the option of inviting local leaders or experts as guest speakers to discuss the project topic with the class. Students should be sure to coordinate this with the teacher.

Be sure students send follow-up communication, such as sending a follow-up email if they have to leave a voicemail or contact office staff. Encourage students to be polite and persistent in their communication efforts.

Resource: What Is an Annotated Bibliography?

1. Guide students through the components of an annotated bibliography and how to format entries for different types of sources.
2. Provide examples of properly formatted citations for various source types, emphasizing the importance of consistency and accuracy.
3. Encourage students to start a shared document, such as a Google Doc or Microsoft Word file, to maintain their research information.
4. Remind students to consult with their group members to be sure all necessary information is included and accurately documented.

Analyzing the Information You Have Gathered

1. Guide students with the whole class or in groups to work together to analyze the information gathered using the Graphic Organizer: Analyzing Information About the Problem.
2. Emphasize the importance of being selective and including only relevant information related to the problem.

Developing a Portfolio and Presentation

1. Guide students in categorizing the information from their annotated bibliographies and discussing its implications for understanding the problem.
2. Organize the class into four groups, each assigned to work on one of the following tasks:
   - Group 1: Explain the problem
   - Group 2: Evaluate alternative policy solutions
   - Group 3: Develop a public policy solution
   - Group 4: Develop an engagement plan

Graphic Organizer: Analyzing Information About the Problem

1. Make sure students understand instructions for each group's task, ensuring they understand their responsibilities and objectives.
2. Be sure groups brainstorm ideas, analyze information, and develop comprehensive responses.
3. Remind students to refer to their research findings, including the annotated bibliography and the Graphic Organizer: Analyzing Information About the Problem, to guide their work on developing the portfolio and presentation.

Extension Activity—Graphic Organizer: Survey-Writing Guide

This research phase provides a good opportunity to teach students about primary and secondary sources, fact and opinion, and the reliability of different types of resources. General research skills, media-literacy skills, survey skills, and interviewing skills may also be taught as needed during this step.

- Teachers may teach a mini lesson on phone skills by requiring students to practice their phone calls by role-playing the call in front of the class with another student. Students should use the Introducing Yourself for an Interview resource in the student edition as a model for the role-play. This activity prepares students for making professional phone calls and demonstrates the importance of being prepared with questions before making a call. Encourage students to ask questions of their own, as well as those in the "Introducing Yourself for an Interview" resource. Stress the importance of coordinating the research tasks so that no more than one student calls each contact.

- If students plan on conducting a survey, which may be useful in determining the scope of the problem, the teacher should teach students the basic principles of conducting surveys before they write one. Explain to students that surveys are useful to find out a small amount of information from a large number of people, whereas interviews are good for finding out a large amount of information from a small number of people. Students should conduct both interviews and surveys in researching their problem. The Graphic Organizer: Survey-Writing Guide in the appendix of this guide has been included to help students write reliable surveys.

- Media literacy is now a crucial component of navigating our digital world. Please see Appendix C for eight discrete lessons on media literacy that can be incorporated throughout Project Citizen.

- Your school librarian may be able to teach lessons on research skills, plagiarism, and citations. Use the graphic organizer and student resources for the annotated bibliography to help give students guidance on the format for citations. Stress the importance of good note-taking and documenting sources of information.

Find It on **Page 57** of the Student Edition

Is All Media Biased?

1. Pose the media-literacy question, "Is all media biased?"
2. Encourage students to share their answers out to the class.
3. In small groups or as a whole class, have students read this section.
4. Divide students into trio teams/small groups.
5. Instruct each group to gather a selection of media samples related to the chosen public issue for their Project Citizen project.
6. Provide guidance on the types of media to include, such as news articles, television clips, social-media posts, and online articles.
7. Encourage groups to analyze each media sample together using the following questions:
   A. What information is presented and how is it presented?
   B. Identify the most persuasive words and techniques used.
   C. Determine the viewpoints or opinions the creator is trying to convey.
   D. Discuss how the type of media influences different interpretations.
8. Facilitate discussions within the groups, ensuring that all members participate and contribute insights.
9. Encourage students to support their observations and insights with examples from the media samples.
10. Prompt groups to summarize their findings within their groups.
11. Provide opportunities for groups to present their summaries to the class.

Teaching Suggestions

- Offer additional support to groups by providing examples of media samples related to the public issue beforehand.
- Consider assigning specific roles within each group, such as a note-taker, discussion facilitator, and timekeeper, to ensure effective collaboration.
- Allow flexibility.

Can I Identify Reliable Information?

1. Pose the media-literacy question, "Can I identify reliable information?"
2. Encourage students to share their answers out to the class.
3. In small groups or as a whole class, have students read this section.
4. Instruct students to select one media source, such as a news website, social-media post, or video, reporting on their Project Citizen public policy issue or a concern in their community or the world.
5. Encourage students to explore how the chosen media source presents information and perspectives on the selected issue.
6. Introduce the ESCAPE Misinformation strategy and explain its components: Evidence, Source, Context, Audience, Purpose, and Execution.
7. Guide students to apply the ESCAPE criteria to evaluate the selected media source:
   A. Evidence: Can the facts be confirmed as true?
   B. Source: Who produced it, and is the source trustworthy?
   C. Context: Can it be verified with another trusted source?
   D. Audience: Who is the intended audience?
   E. Purpose: Why was it created?
   F. Execution: How and when was it presented?
8. Facilitate group discussions where students evaluate the strengths and weaknesses of the media source based on the ESCAPE criteria.
9. Encourage students to share their findings with the class, highlighting key insights and lessons learned from the ESCAPE Misinformation process.
10. Provide opportunities for peer feedback and further discussion on the evaluation process and its implications for media literacy.

Teaching Suggestions

- Model the application of the ESCAPE Misinformation strategy with an example media source before students begin their evaluations.

Do I Play A Role in Staying Safe Online?

1. Pose the media-literacy question, "Do I play a role in staying safe online?"
2. Encourage students to share their answers out to the class.
3. In small groups or as a whole class, have students read this section.
4. Ask students, "How can we identify online safety risks and encourage responsible online behavior?"
5. Divide the class into trio teams/small groups.
6. Direct students to analyze the list of common online safety risks from the word bank. Encourage students to research any unfamiliar terms using digital sources or other references to ensure understanding.
7. Instruct each team to read each scenario and discuss which online safety risk it represents. Have groups write the corresponding risk next to each scenario on their chart.
8. Guide students to brainstorm strategies for promoting responsible online behavior and prevention strategies for each identified risk. Encourage them to consider actions such as setting strong passwords, using privacy settings, and reporting inappropriate content or behavior.

Teaching Suggestions

- Provide examples and real-life scenarios related to online safety to facilitate group discussions and help students apply their knowledge in practical contexts.
- Monitor group interactions and offer guidance as needed to ensure all students actively participate in identifying risks and brainstorming solutions.
  - Possible answers include the following:

Online Safety Word Bank

- Phishing
- Identity Theft
- Cyberbullying
- Inappropriate Content
- Privacy Concerns

Online Safety Risk	Scenario	Prevention Strategy
Privacy Concerns	You receive a message from someone you do not know. They want to see your photos and ask for your phone number. What should you do?	• Only accept friend requests from people you know. • Do not share personal information. • Review your privacy settings online to control who can see your photos and information.

Continued on the Next Page →

Media Literacy Moment

← **Continued From the Previous Page**

Online Safety Risk	Scenario	Prevention Strategy
Inappropriate Content	While searching for a school project online, you come across a website with violent images and offensive language. What actions can you take to deal with this?	● Close the website immediately. ● Report the website to a trusted adult. ● Use parental controls or content filters to block inappropriate content in the future.
Identity Theft	You get an email claiming you have won a prize, but it asks for your personal information like your address and bank details. What should you do?	● Never share personal information, such as your address or bank details, in response to an unsolicited email or message. ● Verify legitimacy of the email by contacting the main email address listed on the organization's official website. ● Be alert and on the lookout for phishing attempts and report them.
Cyberbullying	You receive hurtful messages on social media from someone pretending to be your friend. They start spreading rumors about you online. How would you handle this situation?	● Block or unfriend the person sending the messages. ● Save evidence of the cyberbullying, such as screenshots, and report them to the social-media platform. ● Tell a trusted adult.
Phishing	You receive an email from a bank asking you to update your account information by clicking on a link. How would you verify if it is legitimate or a scam?	● Avoid clicking on links or downloading attachments from unsolicited emails or messages. ● Check for signs of impersonation or suspicious activity.

Do I Have to Cite My Sources?

1. Pose the media-literacy question, "Do I have to cite my sources?"
2. Encourage students to share their answers with the class.
3. In small groups or as a whole class, have students read this section.
4. Direct students to choose two or three sources gathered for their project in their shared document for the annotated bibliography, such as publications, websites, or interviews.
5. For each source, instruct students to write a brief summary explaining why it is relevant to their project. Remind them to keep the summary concise, typically two or three sentences, with subsequent lines indented one-half inch.
6. Provide examples of correct citation formats for different types of sources, such as books, websites, or interviews, as seen in the *Project Citizen* text.
7. Facilitate group collaboration as students work together to create the annotated bibliography. Encourage discussion about the sources and annotations to ensure clarity and accuracy.

Teaching Suggestions

- Support students with research about unfamiliar online safety risks and discuss strategies for promoting responsible online behavior. Encourage them to consider real-life examples.
- Provide examples and templates for creating annotated bibliographies to help students understand the format and structure required for each citation.

4 Developing a Portfolio to Present Your Research

Introductory Note

Step 4 is the most labor-intensive step of Project Citizen. It is in this step that students will conduct the remainder of their research and create a four-part portfolio that explains their project.

There are many ways to structure your classroom during this phase of the project. It is important for all students to learn about each task in the public policymaking process. Therefore, all students should learn about various alternative policies for their topic, how to write their policy, and how to create an engagement plan before dividing into small groups to complete one of these tasks for the final portfolio. These suggested lesson activities provide ideas for teachers to use when teaching about each of the tasks in the policymaking process.

If your class is following the small-group projects model, you can follow the same activities suggested here. Instead of dividing your class into small groups to complete the tasks for the portfolio, however, the small groups will divide up the portfolio task completion work among the people in the group. Each small group will complete an entire portfolio consisting of the four tasks described in these activities.

Purpose

Now that the class has completed Step 3, students are ready to begin developing a portfolio. The portfolio should contain two basic elements: a visual display section and documentation of sources via an annotated bibliography. These elements will each contain four parts corresponding to the four tasks completed at the end of Step 3. The class should be divided into four groups. Each group will be responsible for creating one of the four parts of the portfolio.

If You Are Doing a Whole-Class Project

You may choose to assign students to specific groups or allow them to choose their groups based on their skills, interests, and group members. The following roles may be useful for groups:

- **Project Leader:** Assigns tasks, manages group's timely completion of project
- **Lead Researcher:** Gathers information relevant to group's project topic
- **Reporter:** Writes the main body of the project
- **Designer:** Creates visual elements of project, such as charts and slide decks
- **Quality Controller:** Makes sure all work is accurate and meets quality standards
- **Communication Specialist:** Handles communication with external parties, such as guests and community leaders, also organizes interviews

If You Are Doing Small-Group Projects

Divide students into portfolio task groups based on the topic they are researching for Project Citizen. The following roles may be useful for groups:

- **Coordinator:** Organizes meetings, assigning tasks, and tracking deadlines for project completion
- **Researcher:** Conduct research to make sure project is based on credible sources
- **Content Creator:** Create content to deliver the project using creativity and communication skills
- **Visual Designer:** Design visually appealing presentations and materials for the project

Suggested Teacher Moves

Each of the section headers below correspond to the sections, activities, and resources found in Step 4.

Launching Step 4: Developing a Portfolio to Present Your Research

1. Prompt students to think about the question, "How can we effectively communicate our research findings and solutions?"
2. Encourage students to think about real-world implications of their research and the importance of presenting their ideas in a clear, well-understood way.
3. Divide the class in trio teams/small groups and provide each group with large sheets of paper or digital collaboration tools.
4. Ask groups to brainstorm ideas and strategies for effectively communicating their research findings and proposed solutions.
5. Encourage creative thinking and exploration of different presentation formats, such as visual displays, videos, websites, or interactive infographics.
6. After the brainstorming session, invite each group to share their ideas with the class.
7. Have a discussion on the various communication strategies proposed by the groups, highlighting the strengths and potential challenges of each approach.
8. Remind students to consider factors such as audience engagement, clarity of message, and alignment with project goals.
9. Ask students to reflect individually on the brainstorming session and identify one communication strategy they found particularly compelling.
10. Encourage students to consider how they can incorporate these ideas into their portfolio-development process moving forward.

Portfolio-Development Tasks

1. Review each group's responsibilities one by one, ensuring students understand their tasks and objectives in the "Portfolio-Development Tasks" section of the student edition.
2. Ask students, "What are the key roles and responsibilities of each portfolio group in developing the Project Citizen project?" Allow students time to answer in groups or as a whole class.
3. Follow up with the question, "How can effective collaboration among groups contribute to the success of the overall project?" Allow students time to answer.
4. Emphasize the importance of collaboration and communication among the groups to ensure a cohesive and effective outcome.
5. Provide examples or scenarios to illustrate how each group's work contributes to the overall project.

Specifications for Portfolios

1. Divide the students into their respective portfolio groups (Group 1, Group 2, Group 3, and Group 4).
2. Discuss the specifications for the portfolios outlined in the instructions.
3. Explain that each group will be responsible for creating a section of the portfolio display.
4. Emphasize the importance of organization and clarity in presenting their work.
5. Provide guidance on the types of materials that can be included in each section, such as written statements, lists of sources, charts, graphs, photographs, original artwork, and interactive media.
6. Encourage students to create a visually appealing display with a balanced mix of text and visuals, aiming for approximately 50% text and 50% visuals.
7. Discuss the documentation section and explain that each group should select additional materials to best document their work. This could include an annotated bibliography, digital files, or a documentation binder.
8. Encourage students to use visual dividers, digital subfolders, or panels to separate their work into four sections corresponding to each group's tasks.
9. Remind students to include a table of contents for the documentation of each section to ensure clarity and organization.

Portfolio Evaluation Criteria

1. Guide a discussion on the various methods for presenting research outlined in the document.
2. Explain the advantages and considerations for each method, including poster-board displays, software-based presentations, websites, videos, social media platforms, and interactive infographics.
3. Encourage students to choose a presentation method that best suits their project goals, audience, and resources.
4. Introduce the Project Citizen Portfolio Criteria Checklist to students and explain its significance in guiding the development of their portfolios.
5. Start by explaining the importance of the Project Citizen Portfolio Criteria Checklist in evaluating the quality of each section of the portfolio.
6. Discuss each section of the checklist with the students, ensuring they understand the expectations and criteria for evaluating their work.
7. Divide the class into trio groups. Tell them they are about to play a game to help them understand the Project Citizen Portfolio Criteria Checklist even better.
8. Read out one item from the Project Citizen Portfolio Criteria Checklist at a time without revealing the section it belongs to.
9. After reading each item, allow the groups a few moments to discuss among themselves and decide which section of the portfolio it belongs to.
10. Once the groups have made their decision, they can use their buzzer or signal to indicate they are ready to answer.
11. Call on one group at a time to provide their answer and guess the section of the portfolio the item belongs to.
12. Keep track of the groups' scores and provide feedback and explanations after each guess to ensure understanding.
13. After each guess, reveal the correct section of the portfolio to the class and discuss why the item belongs to that particular section.
14. Discuss the role of judges in evaluating portfolios for simulated public hearings, emphasizing the importance of meeting the criteria for a successful presentation.

Extended Game Instructions for the Portfolio Criteria Checklist

1. While playing the game referenced above to help students understand the Project Citizen Portfolio Criteria Checklist, consider taking the opportunity to reinforce the roles and responsibilities outlined in the "Instructions for Groups" section.

2. Encourage groups to think about how each item on the checklist relates to their assigned roles and tasks within the group.

3. Provide each group with a copy of the Instructions for Groups in the student edition and ask them to discuss the responsibilities and tasks associated with their assigned roles.

4. Direct each group to assign one of the roles mentioned in the Instructions for Groups (Coordinator, Researcher, Content Creator, Visual Designer) for each group member.

5. If available, provide examples or models of well-designed portfolios to illustrate key concepts and criteria.

6. Encourage students to consider the overall design, creativity, and originality of their portfolios in addition to the specific checklist items.

7. Allow time for students to plan and prepare their portfolios.

Teaching Suggestions

To teach students what their finished portfolios should look like by getting students to assess other projects before they begin creating their own. Students can evaluate previous Project Citizen portfolios. If you have portfolios from past years you can share them and allow students to rate them. You can view examples on the Center for Civic Education's website (https://www.civiced. org/project-citizen/resources#portfolios). Provide students with the rubric that you will use to assess their portfolios.

Portfolio Group 1: Explaining the Problem

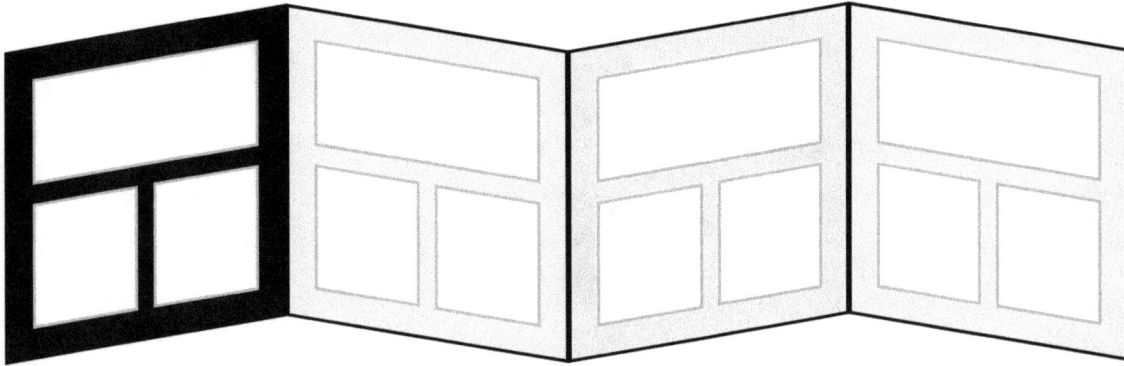

Purpose

Portfolio Group 1 is tasked with explaining the problem in the first display and documentation sections of the portfolio. It is important to note that most tasks for Portfolio Group 1 were completed in Steps 1–3. This group's focus still needs to be on a well-written summary of the problem and thorough documentation of the problem.

If You Are Doing a Whole-Class Project

Make sure that all students are actively engaged by assigning roles and responsibilities to each student. Regular check-ins and review sessions can help all students stay on track.

- Possible Responsibilities:
  - Project Leader: Assigns tasks, manages groups timely completion of project
  - Lead Researcher: Lead gathering on information relevant to group's project topic
  - Reporter: Writes the main body of the project
  - Designer: Creates visual elements of project such as charts, slide decks
  - Quality Controller: Makes sure all work is accurate and meets quality standards
  - Communication Specialist: Handles communication with external parties such as guests and community leaders, also organizes interviews

If You Are Doing Small-Group Projects

Encourage students to divide tasks equally (see page 63).

- Coordinator
- Researcher
- Content Creator
- Visual Designer

Written Summary of Problem

1. Review material gathered by research groups and write a concise summary of the problem.
2. Limit the summary to 500 words and address key questions, such as the severity, scope, existing policies, community disagreements, stakeholders, and government responsibility.
3. Include visual representations of the problem, such as charts, graphs, photos, political cartoons, or newspaper headlines.
4. Each illustration should have a caption or title and a source citation where appropriate.

Documentation Section 1

1. Create an annotated bibliography of the most important sources used in examining the problem.
2. Include citations for all sources used and provide brief annotations summarizing the relevance and credibility of each source.
3. Include selected news screenshots or clippings, reports of community interviews, media coverage, communications from interest groups, and excerpts from government publications.

Portfolio Group 2: Examining Alternative Policies

Purpose

The goal of Portfolio Group 2 is to research and analyze different ways a problem could be addressed through public policy. This includes examining existing policies and proposals put forward by various political parties, interest groups, elected officials, or citizens. It's important to emphasize the value of researching, discussing, and debating the advantages and disadvantages of alternative policies before deciding on the best approach to address the problem.

If You Are Doing a Whole-Class Project

Students may form groups based on the alternative policies they have found. They could do a jigsaw-style learning activity in which students first form groups with others who found the same policy, and then discuss and analyze the policy until all group members understand it well. Students then move into groups with students who found other policies.

Only have students move on to the task for Portfolio Group 3 when all students have completed their research and analysis of alternative policies. To engage students in understanding this step, consider discussing alternative policies that have been proposed to address a current problem other than the one students selected for this project. You can use ongoing issues like poverty, drug abuse, illegal immigration, and violent crime as examples. Show excerpts of congressional debates on C-SPAN (be sure to have on closed captioning) or have students identify online articles that demonstrate the importance of alternative policy debate to American democracy.

If You Are Doing Small-Group Projects

You may also have students present their completed Task 2 to the class at this time. This encourages students to avoid procrastinating until the end of the entire process, and gives them a deadline for completing the second major task. Also, in-class presentations of each task allow the teacher to give students constructive feedback and monitor their progress. These initial presentations will reveal whether a student is doing his or her part in the group and enable the teacher to intervene early in the process. Initial presentations are also productive in allowing students to see the work of other groups, provide constructive feedback, and learn about the problems that other groups are studying.

Written Summary of Problem

1. Identify two or three alternative public policies for dealing with the problem. For each policy, summarize your answers to questions like the following: What is the existing public policy or the policy being proposed? What are the advantages and disadvantages of this policy?

2. Graphic Presentations of the Policies: Include charts, graphs, photos, drawings, political cartoons, news headlines, or tables of statistics related to the policies. Each illustration should have a caption or title and a source citation where appropriate.

3. Identification of Sources: Include an annotated bibliography identifying all sources used.

Documentation Section 2

Regardless of the presentation format, create a documentation section that includes an annotated bibliography of the most important information gathered and used in your examination and explanation of the problem. Additionally, include selected news screenshots or clippings, written reports of interviews with people in the community, media coverage of the problem, communications from public and private interest groups, and excerpts from government publications.

Be prepared to share your annotated bibliography featuring any information important for this section of the portfolio.

Teaching Suggestions

For a Whole-class Project

1. Write on the board or project: "Problem: Drug Abuse. Write three different ways government could or does address this problem." (Choose another problem for this activity if some of your students are studying drug abuse as their Project Citizen problem.)

2. Discuss student answers and write them on the board under the heading "Alternative Policies." Answers should include laws criminalizing possession and distribution of drugs in the United States, anti-drug ad campaigns and education, foreign policy that attempts to control the production of drugs in other countries, rehabilitation centers and therapy for addicts, etc. Discuss student opinions about the advantages and disadvantages of each of these policy proposals and the importance of ongoing debate about policy solutions to America's drug abuse problem.

3. Students conduct research to identify alternative policies that address their chosen problem. You may ask students to formulate a plan for finding these alternatives before they begin researching. As with the task for Portfolio Group 1, research groups may focus on different types of research (internet, newspapers, interviews, etc.), or you may structure this research in a different way. Each student should be asked to find at least one alternative policy individually before the next class meeting.

For Small-Group Projects

As student groups discuss alternatives and complete the chart in groups, walk around the room and make sure groups are completing the chart and allowing each student to share his or her alternative policies. This is a good time to check for individual accountability by checking that each student has found and analyzed an alternative policy.

Portfolio Group 3: Proposing a Public Policy

Purpose

For this section, Portfolio Group 3 will propose a public policy that addresses the problem identified by the class. A majority of the class, or the small group, must agree that this is the best policy to address the problem. This task also provides an opportunity for the teacher to teach about the limits placed on government in our state and federal constitutions. Students must propose a policy that does not violate the U.S. Constitution or their state's constitution. In creating their policy proposal, students may choose to

- support one of the alternative policies identified by Portfolio Group 2,
- modify one of those policies,
- combine aspects of several of the alternatives, or
- develop their own public policy.

At this point, students need to reach consensus on a policy proposal that most students agree is the best way to address the problem. The degree of difficulty for reaching consensus will vary based on the dynamics of your class and how much agreement or disagreement already exists over how to address the problem. The following suggestions may be adapted and used as necessary to help a class identify one policy that will best address the problem:

If You Are Doing a Whole-Class Project

1. As a class, challenge students by asking them exactly how their proposals would work, how much they might cost, and who might not support the policy.
2. Narrow the field of policy proposals through this discussion.
3. Have each student write an individual policy proposal that explains the policy he or she thinks best addresses the problem.

4. When all students have written their individual policy proposals, put students in groups with others who proposed the same basic policy. In these groups, students should discuss their policy proposals and agree on the specifics of their policies.
5. Allow each group to propose its policy to the class, explaining all the advantages and disadvantages in detail. Each group of students should tell the rest of the class if they really think their group's policy proposal is the best way to address the problem.

6. After all groups have presented, conduct a class discussion about the policy proposals, ending in a decision-making process to select one policy or combine elements of various groups' policies. Two ideas for decision-making are voting and the consensus-building method described of this guide.

7. Once students have agreed on a policy, they should evaluate its constitutionality. This step provides an opportunity to teach about the details of your state's constitution and the U.S. Constitution. At a minimum, students should each read the Graphic Organizer: Instructions for Constitutional Opinion and complete it on the student edition.

8. Students' policy proposals and the Graphic Organizer: Constitutional Opinion should be reviewed and given to the students in Portfolio Group 3 for later use in constructing their part of the portfolio.

If You Are Doing Small-Group Projects

1. Follow the same basic lesson plan as suggested for whole-class projects, but adapt the activity so that each small group is deliberating and discussing various policy proposals instead of the entire class doing it together. It is usually easier for small groups to quickly reach consensus on their policy proposals than it would be for an entire class. The key to success with small groups is for the teacher to maintain adequate oversight so that students propose realistic, detailed, and thoughtful policies. You may want to give each group a large sheet of chart paper.

2. On the chart paper, groups can write the key elements of each student's policy proposal.

3. When students have finished their individual policy proposals and summary statements, they should work on their assigned responsibility for completing the task for Portfolio Group 3.

Remind students to refer to the "Sharing the Work" graphic organizer, to see who does what. Completing this task may take at least one class period after the completion of the above activities.

4. You may also have Portfolio Group 3 present their completed task to the class at this time. This encourages students to avoid procrastinating until the end of the entire process and gives them a deadline for completing the third major task. Also, in-class presentations of each task allow the teacher to give students constructive feedback and monitor their progress. These initial presentations will reveal whether a student is doing his or her part in the group and enable the teacher to intervene early in the process. Initial presentations are also productive in allowing students to see the work of other groups, provide constructive feedback, and learn about the problems that other groups are studying. The teacher should ask challenging questions about students' policy proposal, the Constitutional Opinion graphic organizer, the level and branch of government involved, and the cost and feasibility of proposed policies.

5. Encourage students to change some details of their policy proposals if necessary.

Policy Justification Statement

Students should create a statement justifying their policy choice and why it is the best public policy they considered to address the problem they are working to solve. Some students may struggle with the written summary and may need a paragraph frame. Here are two examples.

Paragraph Frame for Justification Statement

Our class has developed a public policy to address [describe the problem]. This policy is aimed at [state the primary goal or objective of the policy]. We believe this policy is necessary because [briefly explain the main reason for the policy]. The problem we are trying to solve is [provide a detailed description of the problem]. This issue is important because [explain why the problem is important and who it affects]. For example, [provide a specific example or statistic to show why it is a problem]. One of the advantages of this policy is [describe the first advantage]. This is an advantage because [explain why this policy is a better solution and why alternatives are less effective]. Compared to alternative policy solutions, this policy is a better solution because [explain why this policy is better]. This is an advantage because [describe second advantage]. Additionally, there are other benefits [mention any other benefits], helping to [explain how these benefits contribute to solving the problem]. However, there are some potential disadvantages to this policy. One disadvantage is [describe the first disadvantage]. This is a disadvantage because [explain why this is a disadvantage]. Additionally, [mention another disadvantage], which might [explain the negative impact]. Despite these challenges, we believe the advantages outweigh the disadvantages because [provide a justification for why the policy is still a good solution]. We strongly believe that implementing this policy will lead to [describe the desired outcome or improvement].

Documentation Section 3

1. Create an annotated bibliography of the most important sources used in examining and explaining the problem.
2. Include citations for all sources used and provide brief annotations summarizing the relevance and credibility of each source.
3. Include selected news screenshots or clippings, reports of community interviews, media coverage, communications from interest groups, and excerpts from government publications.

Alternate Activity
For Using the Constitutional Opinion
Graphic Organizer

1. Begin by providing a brief overview of the U.S. Constitution and its importance in shaping government policies.
2. Discuss the key principles outlined in the Constitution, such as protecting individual rights and ensuring governmental limitations.
3. Divide students into trio teams/small groups and assign each group a specific constitutional right outlined in the graphic organizer (e.g., freedom of expression, due process of law).
4. Have each group discuss and research their assigned right, focusing on its significance, historical context, and legal implications.
5. Present students with hypothetical scenarios that challenge constitutional rights, such as a controversial government policy or a civil liberties case.
6. In their groups, students analyze each scenario, identify potential constitutional issues, and discuss how the rights outlined in the graphic organizer might apply.
7. Distribute copies of the Graphic Organizer: Constitutional Opinion to each group and guide them through a close examination of its sections.
8. Be sure to have students annotate the form, highlighting key terms, questions, and constitutional principles.
9. Lead a whole-class discussion focusing on each section of the form, clarifying any confusing terms or concepts.
10. Use examples to illustrate how the graphic organizer applies to real-world situations.
11. Task each group with analyzing their proposed public policy in relation to the constitutional principles outlined in the form.
12. Provide guidance and support as students work together to assess how their policy aligns with constitutional rights and limitations.
13. Have each group draft a summary statement for their proposed policy, incorporating insights gained from the graphic organizer and group discussions.
14. Hold peer review sessions where groups exchange their summary statements and provide feedback to each other.

Extension Activity
You may invite policymakers into your classroom at this point to discuss with students how policies are written at their level of government. School board members, city council members, state and federal congressional staff members, and other policymakers should be invited to come to class, explain how they write policies, and share examples of real policies they have recently written or voted on. Lessons on the specific structure of policy writing may be emphasized, as well as the lesson that "the devil is in the details" when writing policy. This will help students understand that they may have a good idea for a policy, but that it must be written in a specific way in order to have a real chance of being implemented.

Portfolio Group 4: Developing an Engagement Plan

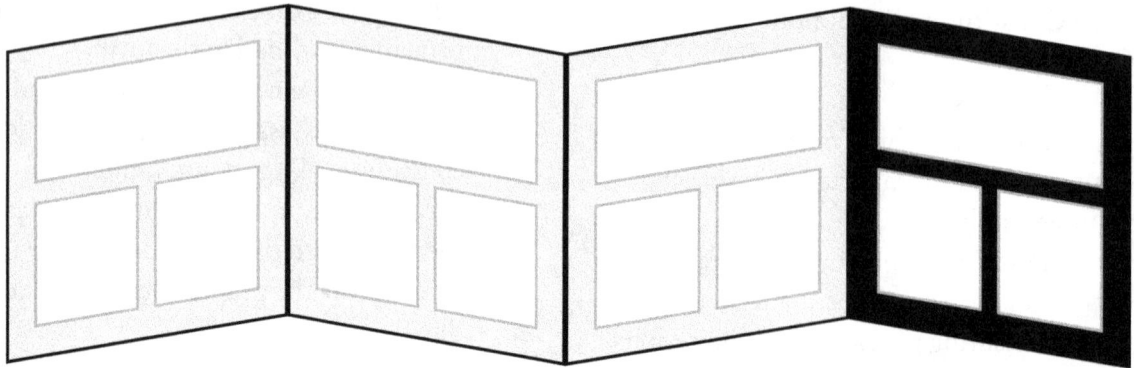

Purpose

For this section, Portfolio Group 4 will develop an engagement plan for gaining support among individuals, groups, and government that will make it possible to get the proposed public policy adopted and implemented by government. The plan should include all the steps that would be necessary. Students will explain the engagement plan in the display section and in the documentation section of their portfolio as described in the student edition.

This task provides an opportunity to teach students many useful and authentic skills, including writing formal emails/letters, petitions, press releases, and advertising copy. The teacher should decide how much time and what priority level to give to each of these skills. Guidelines may be found online, through local professionals, or provided in class as necessary. Just remember that if you want the students to produce professional results in these areas, you must teach them how.

It is important to emphasize the authenticity of this task. Groups and individuals who want specific public policies implemented actually develop engagement plans very similar to what students develop in completing this task. Furthermore, the teacher must decide what level of authenticity he or she expects of students in the engagement plan task. You may have students draft a plan that could gain the support and attention of public policymakers, but not expect students to actually carry out any of the actions. As an alternative, you may suggest that students carry out the steps they explain in their engagement plans. This option is especially useful if your goal is for students to interact with the public and potentially achieve success in getting their policy implemented. This takes more time, but also provides students with a more empowering experience than simply proposing the action but not acting on it.

If You Are Doing a Whole-Class Project

Make sure that all students are actively engaged by assigned roles and responsibilities to each student. Regular check-ins and review sessions can help all students stay on track.

- Possible Responsibilities:
  - Project Leader: Assigns tasks, manages groups timely completion of project
  - Lead Researcher: Lead gathering on information relevant to group's project topic
  - Reporter: Writes the main body of the project
  - Designer: Creates visual elements of project such as charts, slide decks
  - Quality Controller: Makes sure all work is accurate and meets quality standards
  - Communication Specialist: Handles communication with external parties such as guests and community leaders, also organizes interviews

If You Are Doing Small-Group Projects

Give students time to work on completing Task 4 in their small groups, including all the components of the portfolio as explained in the student edition. When students have finished this task, they have completed their portfolios and are ready to present their findings in public. You may stage in-class presentations of Task 4 or the entire portfolio at this time. Students may need some time to complete their final portfolios at a high level of quality.

Documentation Section 4

1. Describe how the proposed public policy will gain support among individuals and groups in the community in 250 words.
2. Identify influential individuals and groups in the community and strategies to gain their support.
3. Address potential opposition and tactics to convince them to support the policy.

Written Explanation of Engagement Plan for Government Support

1. Describe strategies to gain support from government officials and agencies for the proposed policy.
2. Identify potential opponents within government and approaches to persuade them to support the policy.
3. Include visual representations of the engagement plan, such as charts, graphs, photos, or political cartoons.
4. Ensure each illustration has a caption and source.
5. Create a bibliography identifying all sources used in developing the engagement plan.
6. Develop an annotated bibliography of sources used in researching and planning the engagement strategies.
7. Provide citations for all sources and brief annotations summarizing their relevance and credibility.
8. Include selected news screenshots, reports of community interviews, media coverage, communications from interest groups, and excerpts from government publications to support the engagement plan.

Suggested Activity for Developing an Engagement Plan

1. Make a list of three to five actions you could take to get your policy implemented by government. Think about how you could gain the support of influential people and groups and how you could get the attention of policymakers and convince them to devote some of their limited time and resources to implementing this policy.

2. Discuss student answers to Step 1 question. Write a list of student ideas for gaining support on the board.

3. Explain the purpose of Task 4 to students.

4. Review "Portfolio Group 4: Developing an Engagement Plan" directions in Chapter 3 of the student edition.

5. Have students develop a specific engagement plan following the guidelines of Portfolio Group 4. Each student should write an engagement plan individually, which the teacher may grade and use as a tool to keep students individually accountable.

6. In order to carry out some of the steps in their engagement plans, students may need mini lessons on writing formal emails or letters, petitioning, writing press releases, etc. Lessons for these activities may be found online. If students include a press release as part of their engagement plan, they may use real press releases found online as a model.

Teaching Suggestions

Invite local policymakers to your classroom to answer student questions about what actions are most effective in gaining their attention. Students should generate a list of ideas for their engagement plans before policymakers come to class. When policymakers visit, students should ask whether their ideas are likely to get the attention of policymakers and get their policy implemented. You may ask policymakers to discuss specific examples of citizen groups that successfully gained policymakers' attention and proposed policies that were actually implemented. These groups may be used as models for developing a successful engagement plan for the class or group policy proposals.

Extension Activity

Students develop a continuum of actions taken by citizen groups to generate public support for a policy. This activity will help students create an appropriate engagement plan that begins with reasonable actions to gain the government's attention and build support for their policy proposal. Students should learn that civil disobedience and other protest-oriented actions have an important place in American democracy, but that these activities should be considered only when other actions have failed to achieve results.

1. Write the following list of actions on the board. Students should read about the various actions and be prepared to explain one action to the rest of the class. Students may need to research these actions using the internet, dictionaries, textbooks, and other sources. The teacher should assign each small group of students an action they will explain to the class.
   - Writing emails/letters to public officials
   - Attending public meetings and proposing policy changes
   - Contacting the media and writing press releases
   - Advocating for a cause
   - Lobbying public officials in person
   - Holding public meetings to gain support for a policy proposal
   - Asking citizens to sign petitions
   - Boycotting specific businesses or government agencies
   - Staging protests and demonstrations against specific government policies or actions
   - Practicing civil disobedience

2. Write the words "First Steps" on the left side of the board at the front of the room and "Last Resorts" on the right side.

3. Once students have read about some strategies in their group, tell each group to come to the board, write its strategy on the board, and explain how the group could use its strategy to get support for its policy. Students should decide where to place the strategy on the continuum line between "First Steps" and "Last Resorts" (see "Continuum of Strategies" below). Draw this line on the board, and emphasize that things like email/letter writing and lobbying should be done early on, whereas civil disobedience and protest are only used as last resorts if all else fails. This is a good opportunity for a history lesson: discuss the American civil rights movement of the 1950s and 1960s. Emphasize that Black Americans in the South had gone through all the first steps to no avail for almost one hundred years before they resorted to the acts of civil disobedience and protest that most Americans associate with that movement today.

4. Have the groups work together to develop a solid engagement plan based on the stakeholders they have identified and the strategies they have learned about today.

Continuum of Strategies for Gaining Support for Your Policy First Steps
- Letters/emails
- Petitions
- Public meetings
- Lobbying
- Media contacts and press releases

Last Resorts
- Protests
- Demonstrations
- Civil disobedience
- Boycotts

Can I Effectively Create and Share Information?

1. Pose the media-literacy question, "Can I effectively create and share information?"
2. Encourage students to share their answers out to the class.
3. In small groups or as a whole class, have students read this section.
4. Ask students to brainstorm a list of things they should consider when making accurate and fair media for a presentation.
   A. Question to pose to students: What sources will you use for your presentation? How will you make sure your information is not biased?
   B. If students are having difficulty answering, guide their thinking: Consider using reputable news sources like the BBC, Reuters, or the Associated Press for current events.
5. Encourage students to share answers with the whole class. Create a list on the board or on a shared digital space.
6. In trio groups, have students record how they can adjust their media content to connect with different groups of people. Have them consider age, cultures, and backgrounds.
   A. Question to pose to students: How will you modify language or visuals for different audiences?
   B. If groups are having difficulty answering, guide their thinking: For an audience of younger kids, you might use cartoon characters, and for a professional audience, you might use data charts or graphs.
7. Have each group share and discuss as a class how these adjustments can be made.
8. Lead a discussion on how to make sure that fair and accurate content is also persuasive to different people.
   A. Question to pose to students: What persuasive techniques can be used to appeal to the values and interests of different audiences?
   B. If students are having difficulty answering, guide their thinking: One technique is to use social media for younger audiences, as they are more engaged with these platforms. For older audiences, you might use more traditional media like television.
9. Have students write down their favorite three strategies and a short description that they heard in the class discussion to support the development of their portfolio.

Teaching Suggestions

- Show students examples of digital portfolios or similar projects to inspire their creativity and give them ideas for content and presentation.

5 Presenting Your Portfolio in a Simulated Public Hearing

Introductory Note

An "Evaluator Message" has been included in the appendix of this guide. This message may be given to policymakers or other individuals who have agreed to serve as evaluators for a Project Citizen showcase.

Some suggestions for final presentation hearings include the following:

- **Simulated Hearing**
  Teachers invite community members to hear student presentations and give feedback. These people could be any local civic-minded individuals willing to play the role of policymaker. Actual policymakers who have expertise or authority over the students' issues make excellent choices. The hearing could be held at school or in a local community or government facility and should be open to the public. This format is most useful for a small number of portfolios, given the time required for each presentation.

- **Authentic Hearings**
  The teacher or students request time on the agenda of an actual government meeting—a regularly scheduled meeting of the school board, city council, county commission, state legislative committee, or other policymaking body. Students should present their portfolios at the meeting of the policymakers who have jurisdiction over their policy proposal so that there is a real possibility that their policy will be adopted.

- **Showcase of Student Work**
  Students present their portfolios to members of the public or roving evaluators and policymakers in a History Day–type setting. Teachers and participants have often likened these showcases to a science fair. Students engage in multiple conversations about their portfolios but do not present in front of a large audience. Students' portfolios could be set up around school or in the library, for example, and the public would be invited to discuss students'

work at a specified time. This method is especially useful if one teacher has multiple groups presenting many different problems.

- **Alternative Formats**

  Students publish a website and elicit comments from policymakers or community members who visit the site. Students have a videoconference with policymakers who are unable to meet with students in person. This format is especially useful for schools in remote areas and for policy proposals at the federal level of government.

Purpose

When students' portfolios are completed, they should prepare to present their work before an audience in a public hearing. This final presentation is often the most memorable and empowering part of a student's Project Citizen experience. As the teacher, you must decide what type of hearing students will present. Your decision should depend on your goals for student learning and the options you have available in your community. Regardless of the hearing format you choose, it should provide students with an authentic experience of how citizens can participate in public hearings. The structure of simulated hearings should be based on the structure of public meetings, where speakers and expert witnesses testify before committees or boards composed of members of the legislative and executive branches of government.

The guidelines for the simulated public hearings explained in the student text, including the 10-minute limit on presentations, are intended to assist teachers in organizing final hearings in a manageable way. These guidelines should be viewed as suggestions, not requirements, and should be adapted to fit your situation as necessary. No teacher should feel constrained by any of the presentation guidelines or suggestions presented here. Do what is best for you and your students in your unique circumstances.

This step provides an opportunity to teach students many valuable lessons, including public speaking skills. Teachers may also want to teach students when and where their local policymakers meet and remind students that these meetings are open to the public. A lesson on the First Amendment's protection of our right to "petition the government for a redress of grievances" could also fit in here.

A Community Leader Message template has been included in the appendix of this guide for your use in soliciting volunteer participation. The message asks whether the community leader would be able to (a) assist in student research, (b) provide information about a current topic of interest to the students, (c) listen to student presentations, or (d) visit the classroom to help students understand an aspect of public policy or government. You may alter the message as needed.

Suggested Teacher Moves

Each of the section headers below correspond to the sections, activities, and resources found in Step 5.

Launching Step 5: Presenting Your Portfolio in a Simulated Public Hearing

1. Ask students, "What group of policymakers should you present your portfolio to in order to get your proposed policy implemented? How can you get this group of policymakers to actually allow you to present your portfolio to them?"

2. Discuss student answers to the question. Discuss the importance of contacting local policymakers and the right of Americans to "petition the government for a redress of grievances."

3. Students read the "Purpose" section for Step 5 in the student edition as a whole group. Have the students discuss the purpose in trio teams/small groups.

What Are the Goals of the Simulated Public Hearing?

1. In small groups or as a whole class, students should read the overview of the goals of the hearing in "What Are the Goals of the Simulated Public Hearing?" in the student edition.

2. Be sure to give students time to view the "Overview of Simulated Public Hearing" chart. Answer any questions students have about the chart.

Overview of a Simulated Public Hearing

1. Overview both "Opening Oral Presentation" and "Follow-Up Questions"

2. Explain the format students will be using for their hearings if you have chosen a different format or time limits. Remind students that it is a good idea to keep their presentations brief and to the point, regardless of the hearing format, so that they do not lose their audience's attention or confuse them.

3. Overview parts D, E, F, and G of the student edition with students so that they have a clear understanding of the hearings at which they will be presenting. If you have a video of past student presentations, it is useful to show it to students at this time. Students may be encouraged to assess the past presentations using the evaluation criteria on the rubric so that they realize what will be assessed during their presentations.

Inviting Local Leaders and Decision Makers

1. Discuss with your students the importance of communicating with community leaders to serve as panel members for your simulated public hearing.

2. Have students brainstorm strategies to ensure their email effectively communicates the purpose and importance of the showcase.

3. Ask students what details should be included in an email. Students should respond with answers such as date, time, location of the event, the purpose of the showcase presentation, the significance of their role as panelists, and any expectations for panelists

4. Provide students with enough time to view and analyze the email and call templates.

5. Encourage students to consider any additional information panelists might need after receiving the invitation email or call. This may include agendas, schedules, and background information.

6. Guide students to brainstorm ways to anticipate and address potential questions or concerns that panelists may have about the showcase presentation. This may include conversations about open discussion.

7. Discuss with students how they will gauge the success of their communication with panelists and adjust their approach if needed.

Teaching Suggestions

Allow students ample time to practice presenting their portfolios. You may want to conduct multiple practice hearings in class, giving constructive feedback each time, before students are expected to present in public.

6 Reflecting on Your Experience

Introductory Note

In Step 6, students embark on a crucial journey of reflection, evaluating the success of their Project Citizen project and their personal growth throughout the process. They explore the definition of success within the context of their project, considering various dimensions beyond mere project outcomes. Students examine how success can manifest in different forms, encompassing not only tangible achievements but also the broader impact on their community and personal development. Through a structured reflection activity, students assess their evolving attitudes toward public policy and their role as active citizens in shaping societal change.

This introspective process allows students to recognize the transformational journey they have undertaken, gaining insights into their strengths, challenges, and newfound perspectives on civic engagement. By engaging in reflective practices, students deepen their understanding of the project's significance and their contributions to fostering positive change within their communities.

Teachers play a crucial role in facilitating this reflective process, providing students with ample time to brainstorm ideas, fostering discussions about their changing attitudes, and emphasizing the importance of introspection in their civic engagement journey.

Purpose

At first glance, it might appear that Project Citizen is almost entirely about procedures or process and that there is very little content to be gained by taking part in the program. By the time students have reached this step in the program, they should be aware that much of the content of Project Citizen is implicit and much is gained from the experiences students have had in fulfilling the tasks of the program.

The value of the knowledge and experience gained may become more apparent if students are called on to reflect on their experiences. By doing so, students should realize, for example, that they have been exercising many of the rights and fulfilling many of the responsibilities of citizens in a democracy. Students have also been expecting public officials to act in accordance with democratic principles, learning about the importance of civil society, and learning the roles and responsibilities of governmental agencies at local, state, or federal levels. This step calls on students to reflect on and record such knowledge and experience in a report in the final section of their documentation binder, labeled "Part 5."

Suggested Teacher Moves

Each of the section headers below correspond to the sections, activities, and resources found in Step 6.

Launching Step 6: Reflecting on Your Experience

1. Ask students, "What is the most important thing you learned from Project Citizen?"
2. Discuss student answers to the question. Write a list of things students learned on the board.
3. In small groups, have students read the "Purpose" section for Step 6 in the student edition. Discuss.

A Note on Success

1. Pose the following questions: "What does success mean to you for your Project Citizen project? How would you measure it?"
2. As a whole class, read "A Note on Success."
3. After reading the section "A Note for Success," ask students whether their definition for success in their Project Citizen project has changed.

Project Citizen Reflection Activity

1. Arrange the students to stand in a straight line, shoulder to shoulder, facing the same direction.
2. Explain to students that they will participate in a perspective activity to explore different viewpoints on various statements related to Project Citizen.
3. Instruct students that if they strongly agree with a statement, they should take a step forward. If they disagree or feel neutral, they should remain where they are. Also, be sure to let students know that it is okay if they do not move during the activity.
4. Read aloud the following series of statements related to Project Citizen.
   A. I used to think that making a difference in my community was too difficult, but now I think I can make a meaningful impact.
   B. I used to think that adults did not care about what students had to say, but now I think they are more open to listening than I realized.

C. I used to think that it was not my responsibility to address community problems, but now I think I have a role to play in shaping positive change.

D. I used to think that public policy was boring and irrelevant to my life, but now I think it is crucial for improving the well-being of my community.

E. I used to think that my voice did not matter in discussions about local issues, but now I think my perspective is valuable and can make a difference.

F. I used to think that our project would not have much impact, but now I think it has the potential to create real change in our community.

G. I used to think that working with others on a project like this would be frustrating, but now I think collaboration can lead to empowering solutions.

H. I used to think that government officials were too busy to listen to students, but now I think they genuinely want to hear our ideas and perspectives.

I. I used to think that civic engagement was something for adults, but now I think it is important for students to get involved in shaping their communities.

J. I used to think that advocating for change was pointless, but now I think it is empowering to take action on issues that matter to me.

5. Once everyone has positioned themselves, provide time for students to reflect.

6. Students who moved forward can share a statement that resonated with them and how their perspective has changed since the beginning of the Project Citizen process. For students who did not move, encourage them to reflect on why the statements did not resonate with them.

7. Have students return to their seats.

Making Connections: Project Citizen Reflection Activity

1. Divide the class into four groups. Try to make sure each group has a balanced mix of students.

2. Assign each group two questions to discuss and record their responses.

3. Instruct students to actively listen and have open discussion.

4. Remind students to record their responses in the Student Reflection: Reflecting on Project Citizen.

5. In addition to their assigned questions, each group should answer Question 9.

6. After all groups are done, each group should share and discuss their responses with the rest of the class.

7. Remind students that the recorded responses of each group should be used as part of their documentation section.

Find It on **Page 109** of the Student Edition

Am I Media Literate?

1. Pose the media-literacy question, "Am I media literate?"
2. Encourage students to share their answers out to the class.
3. In small groups or as a whole class, have students read this section.
4. Ask students to reflect individually on the Project Citizen journey and consider the ways media representations, coverage, and interactions influenced their project experience.
5. Tell students to ask themselves the following questions: "Did the media affect your project? Why or why not?"
6. Select one of the following reflection methods to express your insights creatively:
   A. Creative writing: Write a reflective essay, poem, or short story discussing the impact of media on your Project Citizen project. Reflect on how your understanding of media influenced your understanding of the topic or affected your project's outcomes.
   B. Visual representation: Create a visual representation, such as a poster, collage, or drawing, showcasing how media and your understanding of media influenced your project experience. Use symbols, images, and captions to convey your reflections.
   C. Audio reflection: Record an audio/video reflection or podcast episode discussing the media's role and your understanding of media in shaping your Project Citizen journey. Share personal stories, examples, and reflections on media influence.
7. Have students share your reflection with classmates or project team members.
8. Lead a discussion about the influence of the media on the Project Citizen project. Record any themes among students.
   A. Be sure to discuss the strengths and limitations of media platforms, the influence of different media narratives, and the ethical responsibilities of media producers and consumers.

Teaching Suggestions

- Discussion Prompts: Offer discussion prompts or guiding questions to facilitate group discussions about media impact. Encourage students to explore topics such as the influence of media bias, the role of social media in shaping public opinion, and strategies for discussing media.

4 Why Is My Participation Important to Democracy?

Purpose

The purpose of this final step is to help students understand why participation is important to democracy. Students will discuss the importance of participation, how people can participate and continue the kind of informed engagement practiced in Project Citizen, and make commitments to continue their informed engagement.

Suggested 5E Inquiry Lesson Plan

Engage

1. Ask students, "Would our country be better off if more people participated in the democratic process the way we have during Project Citizen?" Encourage them to explain their answers.

2. Discuss student answers to the question. Encourage students to consider the consequences of refusing to participate in a democratic system of government.

3. Share the compelling question for Chapter 4: "Why is my participation important to democracy?" Give students time to answer the question in trio groups.

4. Ask students to read silently or in trio teams the "Purpose" section of Chapter 4. Ask a follow-up question: "What do you think is the main idea or purpose of Chapter 4 based on what you read?"

5. Share supporting question 1: "How can I continue my informed engagement in my community?" Ask students how they might continue or extend their engagement in their Project Citizen public policy after the school year ends.

6. In small groups or as a whole class, have students read the section, "How Can I Continue My Informed Engagement in My Community?"

7. Have students research other public policy issues related to their Project Citizen topic. For example, the overuse of pesticides impacts the honeybee population. Without these pollinators, crops and our food supply are in danger. A food shortage could impact health.

Explore

1. Share supporting question 2: "How can I continue to have an informed opinion?"

2. Ask students to connect to the discussion of the importance of citizen participation in our government.

3. In small groups or as a whole class, have students read the "How Can I Continue to Have an Informed Opinion?" section.

4. In small groups, ask students these questions based on what they have read: "How would you answer supporting question 2 in regard to your Project Citizen project? How can you continue the goals of their project outside the bounds of school? Outside of the school year? After completing high school?"

5. Ask students to generate a list of ways to continue the aim of their projects.

6. Students explore these options and commit to doing one.

7. Encourage students to share out in trios/team groups.

Explain

1. Ensure each student has a copy of Making Connections: Roles for Participation in Democracy—Now What Do You Think? Remind students of the questions they answered in Chapter 1 and emphasize that they should not look back at their previous responses before completing the activity. We recommend students do the Making Connections: Roles for Participation in Democracy as the Explain activity, even though it comes after the Collaborate Together: Roles and Responsibilities of Citizens activity because it lends itself to student discussion and dialogue.

2. Instruct students to individually answer the questions in Making Connections: Roles for Participation in Democracy—Now What Do You Think? based on their current understanding and experiences after completing the program.

3. Encourage students to provide thorough explanations for their answers, drawing upon the knowledge gained from the program.

4. After students have completed the questions, have them compare their current responses to their answers from Chapter 1.

5. Divide students into small groups to facilitate collaborative discussion. Encourage students to discuss any changes in their perspectives, insights gained, or areas where their views remain consistent.

6. Facilitate a whole-group discussion where students can share their reflections and engage in dialogue about the evolution of their understanding of citizenship and democracy.

7. Conclude with a reflection period where students can contemplate the impact of their participation in the Project Citizen program on their views and attitudes toward citizenship and democracy.

Elaborate

1. In small groups or as a whole class, have students read the "Conclusion" section of Chapter 4.

2. Encourage students to reflect on their personal growth in citizenship throughout the project. Ask, "How have you grown in your understanding and practice of citizenship throughout the Project Citizen process?" Encourage students to think of specific examples or experiences. Some responses you can anticipate include the following:
   A. Better understanding of responsibilities of citizens
   B. Awareness of civic issues
   C. How to make change through public policy
   D. How to effectively correspond with community, civic, and political leaders
   E. How to communicate better within a group
   F. The changes youth can make in their communities

3. Review with students the Collaborate Together: Roles and Responsibilities of Citizens activity in the student edition.

4. Divide the class into groups of six students each.

5. Make sure each group has access to the quotations related to citizens' roles and responsibilities.

6. Ensure that each group has a blank sheet of paper or a large sticky note for writing their reflections and findings.

7. At each station, students will respond to the questions related to the quotations provided in the student edition using the blank sheet of paper or large sticky notes.

8. Instruct each group to locate their assigned quotation in the student edition and read it together.

9. Have groups discuss and answer the questions related to their assigned quotation, referring to the student edition for guidance. Encourage students to use evidence or examples to support their answers.

10. Encourage students to engage in thoughtful discussion and collaboration to answer the questions about their quotations.

11. Once each group has discussed their quotation and answered the questions, have them hang up their written reflections in clear sight, either on their desks or the walls around the class space.

12. Conduct a gallery walk where student groups visit each station to observe each group's poster.

13. Tell students to write a "+1" next to any statements that resonated with them or a "?" next to any statements where they need more clarification.

14. Instruct students to rotate to each station in the classroom to read about the assigned quotations and that group's analysis.

15. Invite students to write down any additional questions that arise as they read through each group's responses on remaining sticky notes.

16. Gather the class together after the gallery walk is completed.

17. Facilitate a discussion where students can share their reflections, findings, and any questions they have from the gallery walk.

18. Encourage students to discuss similarities and differences between the quotations and their interpretations.

Teaching Suggestions

1. Break down each step: consider breaking down the gallery-walk activity into smaller, more manageable steps to ensure clarity and understanding for students.

2. Use student repetition: utilize the strategy of asking students to repeat the directions back to you to ensure comprehension. After explaining each step of the gallery walk, prompt students to summarize the instructions in their own words or ask them to repeat key points.

Evaluate

1. Encourage students to reflect on the project they worked on during Project Citizen.

2. Pose the following questions:
   A. What immediate actions can you take to continue addressing the issue you focused on during Project Citizen?
   B. Within the next few months, what steps can you take to further advance your project or contribute to ongoing efforts in your community?
   C. What long-term commitments are you willing to make to sustain your engagement and advocacy beyond the duration of the project?

3. Make sure each student has access to Student Reflection: Recording Your Commitments to Informed Engagement.

4. Instruct students to reflect on their Project Citizen project and record their immediate, mid-term, and long-term commitments to continue their informed engagement in their community.

Extension Activity

1. Students create a top-five list ranking the quotations in Collaborate Together: Roles and Responsibilities of Citizens in order of importance.

2. Students can create a short video/audio clip drawing connections between one of the quotations and their selected public policy issue.

APPENDICES

Appendices

APPENDIX A
SUPPLEMENTARY MATERIALS FOR INSTRUCTION

Understanding Foundational Principles

Instructions: Read your assigned foundational principle. Write the main idea, findings, and insights about your principle in the corresponding chart below. Discuss in small groups whether you see similarities and differences in the principles. Add any similarities and differences your group found to the chart.

Principle	Classical Republicanism	Classical Liberalism	Federalism	Popular Sovereignty	Representative Government
Main Idea					
What Is Similar and What Is Different?					
Examples					

Something I found surprising about the five foundational principles was ...

Spheres of Society

In small groups, read through each problem and determine which of the three parts of society should be primarily responsible for dealing with the problem from Collaborate Together: Whose Responsibility Is It?

Private Sphere	Civil Society	Government

Know, Wonder, Learn

Take a moment to reflect and complete the chart to share your impressions.

What Do You KNOW About This Topic? (K)	What Do You WONDER About This Topic? (W)	What Have You LEARNED About This Topic? (L)

Triangle, Square, Circle

Evaluate your understanding of public policy by completing this exit ticket.

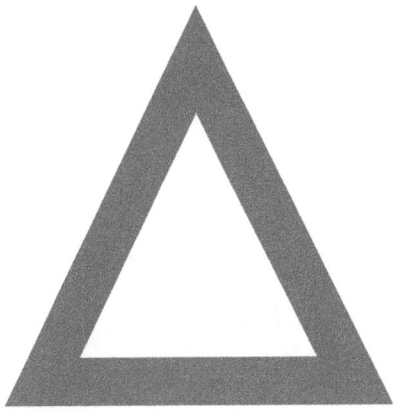

Write three points you learned about public policy today next to the triangle.

Write something next to the square that "squares" with you—the topic makes sense and seems important— related to the question: "Do we need public policy?"

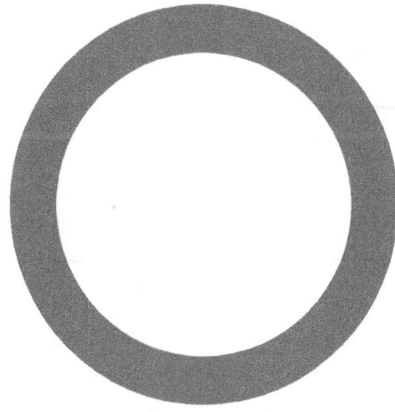

Write a question that is still circling with you about public policy, such as, "Which sphere is responsible for addressing an issue?," "Is there a difference in the three spheres?," or "What kinds of issues are public policy?"

The Four Factors

1. What is the public policy problem you have identified? Explain in detail.

2. Attach an article or summary of an interview that relates to this problem. Explain the main points of the article or interview and how it helps demonstrate that there is a problem.

3. Rate this problem according to the four factors below.
   Use a scale from 1–5, with 1 being very low/few and 5 being very high/many.

	1	2	3	4	5	Why did you give it this score?
Scope						
Intensity						
Duration						
Resources						

Continued on the Next Page →

The Four Factors (continued)

← Continued From the Previous Page

4. What additional information would serve as evidence to policymakers of the severity of the problem in each of the four factors?

Scope (How widespread is the problem?)	
Intensity (How troublesome is the problem?)	
Duration (How long has this been a problem?)	
Resources (What is at stake because of the problem?)	

5. Questions and wonderings about this problem and policy are ...

Survey-Writing Guide

Good surveys can be difficult to write. Follow these steps to improve your chances of yielding accurate information that answers the questions you need answered.

1. Set a main goal that you want the survey to accomplish. What is the main thing you want to know?

2. Write five questions that directly relate to your main goal. Each question should be brief, clear, and unbiased—it should not lead participants to choose one answer over another.

3. Create responses that participants can choose from for each of your questions. Think about how you will tabulate your results into a presentable form as you create your questions and responses. Responses should be multiple choice or a rating scale. Some common rating scales are
   ○ "disagree–agree,"
   ○ "never–always," and
   ○ "poor–excellent."

   If using a numeric scale, higher numbers should represent a more positive or agreeing answer. For each question, include a response option of
   ○ "don't know,"
   ○ "not sure,"
   ○ "don't care," and
   ○ "prefer not to answer," or another way for participants to opt out of the question.

   Add a "Comments" section at the end of the survey.

4. Proofread your survey and, with your teacher's permission, test it by giving it to a few of your classmates before making multiple copies. As your test group takes the survey, make notes on any questions that were confusing and on response options that were not adequate for the participants' true opinions to be explained. Talk to your test group once they complete the survey, and make notes on improvements you need to make.

5. Edit your survey based on the test group's experiences. Write a final draft and then make enough copies to survey a large enough group of people to gain reliable results.

6. Digitally provide the surveys to your target population. You can do this through a number of free platforms, but the most important consideration for your distribution method is to make it as easy as possible for participants to complete and share responses. You will gain more responses if participants can complete the survey and return it to you as soon as they are finished. If you leave surveys with participants and ask them to return the completed forms later, you will usually not get many back.

7. Tabulate your results.

8. Present your results in chart, graph, or text form. Choose only the most conclusive or relevant results to include in your portfolio.

Continued on the Next Page →

Survey-Writing Guide (continued)

← Continued From the Previous Page

1. Main Goal of the Survey

2. Questions that directly relate to your main goal:

Example	How often do you attend town hall meetings?
	☐ Never
	☐ Rarely
	☐ Sometimes
	☐ Often
	☐ Always

Question 1

Question 2

Question 3

Question 4

Question 5

3. How will you tabulate your results into a presentable form?

Project Citizen Research Prompt

1. Today I am going to find out ...

2. Options for how I will start researching this question include (be specific) ...
   -
   -
   -

3. By my next class, I am going to find out ...

4. Options for where I will research information about this question include (be specific) ...
   -
   -
   -

5. I will come to class with ...

6. Questions and wonderings about this problem ...

Continued on the Next Page →

Project Citizen Research Prompt (continued)

← Continued From the Previous Page

During the next class, your group will have to report to the class the following:

1. A clear explanation of the problem
2. The negative effects of the current situation
3. The scope of the problem
   - ☐ Include statistics on how many people are affected by it.
   - ☐ How are they affected?
   - ☐ In what areas—local, state, regional, national, or international—are those who are affected?
4. The intensity or duration of the problem
   - ☐ Who is passionate about this problem?
   - ☐ Who is most severely affected by it?
   - ☐ How long has it been going on?
5. Public policy
   - ☐ Is there a current policy?
   - ☐ What is it?
   - ☐ What resources (money, people, time, space, etc.) are currently dedicated to this problem?

Alternative Policy Summary

1. Where did you find this information about this policy?

2. What is the policy? Does it have a title or name?

3. How does it help solve the problem? Specifically, what does the policy do?

4. Is this policy being used or proposed anywhere? What level of government is involved?

5. Who created this policy? Who supports this policy?

6. What are the advantages of this policy?

7. Who opposes this policy?

Continued on the Next Page →

Alternative Policy Summary (continued)

← Continued From the Previous Page

8. What are the disadvantages of this policy?

9. Do you think this policy would help us solve our problem? Why or why not?

10. Questions and wonderings I still have about this alternative policy are ...

Analyzing Alternative Policies

Type of Policy ▷	
Alternative	
Advantages	
Disadvantages	
Supporters / Opponents	
Things We Need to Find Out About This Policy	

Type of Policy ▷	
Alternative	
Advantages	
Disadvantages	
Supporters / Opponents	
Things We Need to Find Out About This Policy	

Type of Policy ▷	
Alternative	
Advantages	
Disadvantages	
Supporters / Opponents	
Things We Need to Find Out About This Policy	

Portfolio Tasks Organizer

Problem

Describe the ...

Problem:	
The problem's importance:	
The need for a solution:	

Alternative Policies

List three alternative policies and the advantages and disadvantages of each.

Alternative #1

Advantages:	Disadvantages:

Alternative #2

Advantages:	Disadvantages:

Alternative #3

Advantages:	Disadvantages:

Continued on the Next Page →

Portfolio Tasks Organizer (continued)

← Continued From the Previous Page

Proposed Public Policy	
Develop a public policy solution, list its advantages and disadvantages, and suggest what levels of government or agencies should be responsible for implementing the policy. Explain why the proposed policy does not violate the U.S. Constitution or your state's constitution.	

Proposed Policy Solution:	
Level of Government and Agencies Involved:	
Why Is This Policy Constitutional?	

Advantages:	Disadvantages:

Engagement Plan
List the steps your class should take to get government to accept the policy you are proposing.

Project Tasks: Whole-Class Projects

Task:	
Group Members:	

Each panel must have the following:

1. Final Written Summary

Who will do this step?	

- ○ Write one to two pages, typed, double spaced
- ○ Include ideas from many students' papers
- ○ Explain where you got the information

2. Visuals

Who will do this step?	

Visuals help people understand your points.
- ○ Photographs or graphics
- ○ Charts
- ○ Headlines from news sites or newspapers
- ○ Statistics
- ○ Quotes from people
- ○ Examples of surveys, petitions, etc.

3. Construction

Who will do this step?	

Information must be displayed on the panels in a neat, organized way.
- ○ Title
- ○ Captions to explain each visual

4. Construction of Annotated Bibliography

Who will do this step?	

Sources of information used on each portfolio panel must be cited in bibliographic format.
- ○ Bibliography on panel
- ○ Well-organized documentation

Sharing the Work: Small-Group Projects

Problem / Portfolio Title:	
Format of Final Portfolio:	☐ Four-panel display board ☐ Video ☐ Website ☐ Other digital-based presentation
Group Members:	● ● ●

Who is doing what in your group?

Fill in your names below, keep a copy for your group, and return a copy to your teacher.

	Problem	Alternative Policies	Class Policy	Engagement Plan
Written Summary:				
Graphics:				
Bibliography and Documentation:				
Construction:				

Your final group project must include the following:

Four Tasks

1. The problem
2. Alternative policies
3. Proposed public policy
4. Engagement plan

Four Requirements for Each Panel or Step

1. Written summary
2. Graphics
3. Bibliography and documentation binder
4. Construction

Your group may divide up the work in one of three ways:

1. Each student is responsible for a different requirement on each panel.
   Each student will have an opportunity to do each of the four requirements once.
2. Each student is responsible for the same requirement on each panel.
3. Each student is responsible for the entire final product of one panel.

Task Contribution

Explain in detail which tasks you did for your portfolio group. Detail your contributions in each of the following categories.

Research

Construction

Writing

Interviews, Surveys, Correspondence, etc.

Other

Our Proposed Public Policy

The level of government—school, school district, local, county, state, or national—that will best deal with this problem is …

This level of government can best deal with the problem because …

We propose that [level of government] adopt(s) these specific details in its new policy:

-
-
-

The advantages of this policy are …	The disadvantages of this policy might be …
•	•
•	•
•	•

Questions and wonderings I still have about this policy are …

Our Policy Outline

Level of government that will best deal with the problem—school, school district, state, county, or national government

This level of government can best deal with the problem because ...

The decision makers at this level of government are ...

We propose that _____ **[level of government] adopt(s) these specific details in its new** _____ **policy:**

1. _____

2. _____

3. _____

The advantages of this policy are ...

1. _____

2. _____

3. _____

The disadvantages of this policy are ...

1. _____

2. _____

3. _____

Community Leader Message

Dear Community Leader:

I am writing to inform you about and invite you to participate in an exciting civic education project being undertaken by our students. Project Citizen is a curricular program that promotes competent and responsible participation in local, state, and federal government. The program helps young people learn how to monitor and impact public policy. In the process, young people develop an understanding of the democratic principles vital to constitutional democracy and faith in their ability to make a difference in their community.

Small groups of students work cooperatively to identify a public policy problem in their community. They then research the problem, evaluate different solutions, develop their own solution in the form of a public policy, and create an engagement plan to gain support from local, state, or federal authorities to adopt their proposed policy. Participants develop a portfolio of their work and present their project in a hearing showcase before a panel of civic-minded community members or policymakers.

This is where you come in! As students research their issue and search for alternative solutions, they may contact you with questions. If contacted by one of my students, please assist them in obtaining the information they need, while keeping in mind that the students are learning how to research and communicate effectively. Students are required to identify real, current public policy problems. Therefore, they may question you about a contested topic or one about which you have strong views. Please remember that the focus of this project is to instill the civic skills and responsibilities our constitutional democracy requires of its citizens by getting them to participate in their own governance. As leaders and role models for these students, we hope you will support, encourage, and teach them how to be thoughtful community members, even if that requires discussing challenges to our current public policies.

When the students complete their research and analysis, they will identify the level and branch of government that has the authority to implement their proposed policy. They will then make a presentation to that group of policymakers. This is the most memorable and influential stage in this project. Students never forget the time they presented their ideas to a school board, city council, or other civic body. In the interest of efficiency, I would like to schedule a time when multiple groups of students can present their policy proposals to you or a time when a representative from your organization can listen to student presentations at our school. I will contact you with more details about this request as the projects develop.

Continued on the Next Page →

Community Leader Message (continued)

← Continued From the Previous Page

I would like to invite you to visit my classroom as students work on Project Citizen. If you have time to tell students about your job, discuss current public policy issues, explain how policy is made, explain the structure of your agency or government body, or assist students in their research, please email me at [insert email] or call me at [insert phone number]. Our class typically meets at [insert times and days, or dates] and our school is located at [insert school address and room number]. I would love to coordinate a visit with you or your staff at your earliest convenience.

Your participation in this effort is invaluable to its success. I look forward to working with you soon! For more information about Project Citizen, visit **https://www.civiced.org/project-citizen**.

Sincerely,

[Your Name]

Writing a Legislative Bill

Writing the appropriate language for a public policy or a bill can be tricky. Sometimes even the people who serve as state legislators need help. The following guidelines were adapted from the Montana State Legislature's website.* It provides state legislators with a series of questions they need to answer so that the people in the bill-drafting office of the legislature can turn their ideas into a bill, and if passed by the legislature, a law.

Review the 10 questions that the legislators need to answer. The questions can help you as you prepare the class policy that you need when you are working on the third task of portfolio development: proposing a public policy. Although you may not be writing actual legislation for your policy, the questions will help you clarify your thinking about whom and what you should be addressing.

The person who writes the proposed legislation must translate objectives to policies. To do this, all bill drafters must be specific as to what they wish to accomplish and must also outline the method that will achieve that goal. Please use the following questions to help you do so:

1. What exactly is the problem that needs to be solved?
2. Who has experienced the problem—is it perceived as widespread or local in nature?
3. What is the proposed solution to the problem?
4. How should the solution be achieved; that is, what action should government take to intervene in the problem?
5. What results are desired; if the bill passes, what results would show that the solution had been achieved?
6. Who should the person writing the proposed legislation contact for information?
7. Do you know of specific existing statutes that should be changed to achieve your proposed solution?
8. Is there specific legislation from another state, organization, agency, or other source that could serve as a model for your bill? If you think you heard or read about something somewhere, try to find as specific a reference as possible to it: where you learned of it, who said it, when it was said, etc. If you have a copy, please provide it.
9. Does the solution require additional money? How should the money be raised or from what existing source should it come? (Mandates to local governments must authorize a source of funding.)
10. What alternatives to legislation have been considered to solve the problem? Why and how have they failed?

---

* Montana State Legislature: https://leg.mt.gov/content/For-Legislators/Orientation/2020/2020-leg-handbook.pdf.

Self-Evaluation

Use this self-evaluation organizer to reflect on your effort and contributions during the Project Citizen experience. Use the three criteria below for guidelines. Rate yourself on a scale of 1 to 5, with 5 being the highest score.

Participation

I participated without being asked. I shared my strengths and offer to do things I am good at. I contributed to the group's success. *Circle the most appropriate number.*

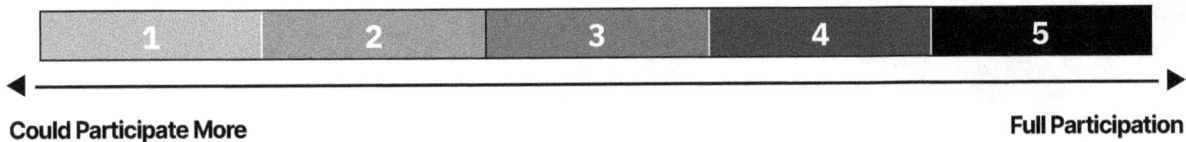

| 1 | 2 | 3 | 4 | 5 |

◄ —— ►

Could Participate More   **Full Participation**

Completion of Assignments

I completed my assignments on time. I came to class prepared every day and did more than expected outside of class. I found solutions to problems and always accomplished my part. I looked for things that needed to be done and did them. *Circle the most appropriate number.*

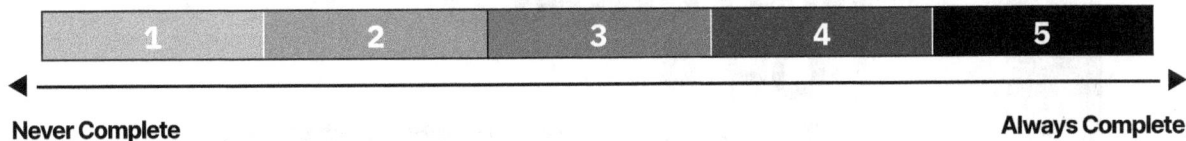

| 1 | 2 | 3 | 4 | 5 |

◄ —— ►

Never Complete   **Always Complete**

Collaborating with Group Members

I worked well with every member of the group. I helped the entire group plan and accomplish goals. I did not boss others around. I practiced active listening and engaged in civil discourse with my classmates. I always worked toward group goals. *Circle the most appropriate number.*

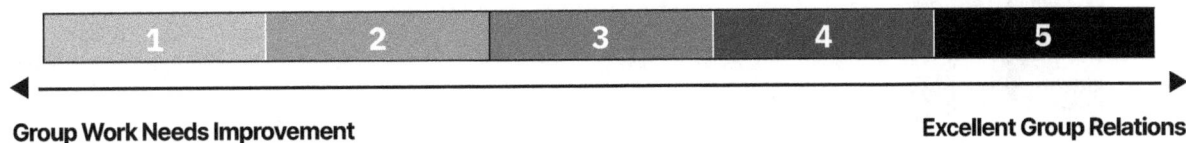

| 1 | 2 | 3 | 4 | 5 |

◄ —— ►

Group Work Needs Improvement   **Excellent Group Relations**

Comments

APPENDIX B
MATERIALS
FOR A
PROJECT CITIZEN
SHOWCASE

Guidelines and Procedures
for Conducting a Showcase Event

These guidelines and procedures represent an effort to provide a consistent structure for national implementation of Project Citizen showcase events. We have attempted to make these guidelines and procedures as clear, concise, and useful as possible. We believe that everyone who participates in the various showcase events at the local, state, and national level will appreciate clearly defined guidelines and uniform procedures and criteria for rating the portfolios and simulated hearing.

Participation

A major objective of Project Citizen is to encourage the widest possible participation from a broad range of students in various types of class settings and with members of youth groups sponsored by community organizations.

Showcase Events

There are two main types of events that comprise a showcase. Both of these events involve members of the community rating the students' level of achievement using the guidelines and rating instruments provided in this guide.

1. **Portfolio Display and Evaluation**
    This event involves members of the community in reading, analyzing, and evaluating the portfolios produced by the students in a class or youth group. Typically, the portfolios are displayed in a prominent public venue and the rating takes place without students being present.

2. **Simulated Hearing**
    This event involves all the students or youth-group members who developed the portfolio. Each of the four groups of students who worked on the four sections of the portfolio are given an opportunity to make oral presentations and respond to follow-up questions from a panel of community members.

Continued on the Next Page →

Showcase Procedure

← **Continued From the Previous Page**

Portfolios

The standard format for a portfolio, as described in the student edition, consists of two major components—a digital or physical display comprising four sections and documentation, again, either digital or physical. Portfolios should still include the basic components described below, regardless of the medium students use to present their work.

Display

The display consists of the following elements:

- Four sections of content displayed digitally or physically on a poster board or something equivalent. Each of the four portfolio groups in the class will have one section to display its work. Each section should include the following:
  - A written summary of the required topics
  - A variety of graphic illustrations
  - An identification of the sources used to gather information
    (See the Graphic Organizer: Annotated Bibliography and instructions.)

Documentation

The documentation consists of the following elements:

- An annotated bibliography comprising a complete list of sources used, with annotations to support the relevance and rationale for each source
  - Copies of the best supporting documentation or research evidence that each group has gathered for its section
  - The class evaluation and reflection on their experience

Simulated Hearings

Oral presentations by participating students in the form of a simulated hearing are an essential part of the Project Citizen learning experience. Teachers are encouraged to include a simulated hearing before a panel of community members to serve as the students' authentic audience. These oral presentations might be made to other classes, caregivers, or community groups, such as a parent–teacher organization, Rotary Club, etc. This activity will provide students with valuable experience in presenting ideas to others and in convincing an audience of a position on a vital public policy issue. Chapter 3, Step 5: Presenting Your Portfolio in a Simulated Public Hearing in the student edition outlines the goals and procedures for the class to use when making oral presentations.

Continued on the Next Page →

← **Continued From the Previous Page**

Goals

- Explain the importance of the problem students have studied.
- Explain and evaluate the advantages and disadvantages of different policies designed to deal with the problem students have selected.
- Explain why students' proposed public policy is the best way to deal with the problem and make the case for adoption and implementation of their proposed policy. In doing so, students should explain why their proposed policy does not violate the U.S. Constitution or their state constitution.
- Explain how students' proposed engagement plan is designed to get governmental officials to adopt and implement their policy.

Procedures

In developing a portfolio and preparing for the simulated hearing, each class or youth group is divided into four portfolio groups—one for each section of the portfolio. Each of the four portfolio groups will present a prepared four-minute statement about its research on the problem it studied. Students will then respond for six minutes to follow-up questions from the panel of community members.

A volunteer serving as a timer will indicate when one minute remains in the prepared testimony and again when one minute remains in the follow-up questioning. Students may use written notes for the four-minute prepared testimony but not for the follow-up questioning period. Students may refer to their portfolio display to emphasize a point at any time during either part of the oral presentation.

Timers

For each simulated hearing showcase, there should be a volunteer who serves as a timer. The timer should not be one of the panel members who will be rating the students' oral presentations. The timer should adhere strictly to the 10-minute framework for each portfolio group presentation: four minutes for prepared testimony and six minutes for the follow-up questioning. Timers will notify the students of the time remaining by holding up a card when they have one minute left in the prepared statement time and again when there is one minute left in the follow-up questioning period. When the full 10 minutes has expired, the timer will stop the presentation by announcing "Time!" Below is an overview of the timing for the public hearing.

Continued on the Next Page →

← **Continued From the Previous Page**

Timing Overview of a Simulated Public Hearing

Presentation Element	Timeframe
Opening Oral Presentation Group 1: Explaining the Problem	Four minutes
Follow-Up Questions Group 1: Engaging in a Dialogue with Panel	Six minutes
Opening Oral Presentation Group 2: Evaluating Alternative Policies to Deal With the Problem	Four minutes
Follow-Up Questions Group 2: Engaging in a Dialogue with Panel	Six minutes
Opening Oral Presentation Group 3: Proposing a Public Policy to Deal With the Problem	Four minutes
Follow-Up Questions Group 3: Engaging in a Dialogue With Panel	Six minutes
Opening Oral Presentation Group 4: Developing an Engagement Plan	Four minutes
Follow-Up Questions Group 4: Engaging in a Dialogue With Panel	Six minutes

Selecting Evaluators

The following points will be helpful as you undertake the task of selecting members of the community to serve as evaluators to rate the students' level of achievement on the portfolios and in the simulated hearing.

For every three portfolios in the showcase event, there should be a panel of three volunteers who will evaluate the students' achievements. These panels should be made up of individuals who are knowledgeable about the policymaking process, current public policy issues, and the link between civic education and civic participation. Evaluators should include prominent and knowledgeable community members from both the public and private sectors. A wide variety of individuals would be ideal to serve as evaluators. Think about inviting some of the following people:

- Active and retired teachers
- College professors
- Elected and appointed public officials
- Journalists
- Lawyers, judges, and law-enforcement personnel
- Members of community organizations (League of Women Voters, Kiwanis Club, Veterans of Foreign Wars)
- Professionals in the field for related project topics (environmental scientist, city planner, researcher, etc.)
- High school students who have previously participated in the Center for Civic Education's programs, like We the People: The Citizen and the Constitution

Continued on the Next Page →

Materials

You will need to provide each evaluator with the following materials:

- Evaluator Guidelines for the Portfolio Showcase
- Project Citizen Portfolio and Hearing Evaluation Sheet found on pages 134–136

If the students are making oral presentations, the evaluators will need the following:

- Evaluator Guidelines for the Simulated Hearing
- Project Citizen Portfolio and Hearing Evaluation Sheet

Preparing Evaluators

Conduct a briefing meeting with the individuals who will serve as evaluators of the students' work. Carefully review the overall goals of Project Citizen. Pay particular attention to the nature of middle school students and the expectations that evaluators should reasonably have for them. In your meeting, review the shared materials above.

Emphasize that evaluators need to give students some positive feedback and offer some constructive suggestions on how students might improve their portfolio and oral presentations. The role of evaluators is not to poke holes in student presentations but to have a conversation about improvements and further questions to explore and to celebrate student learning.

As a general guideline, you will need one panel of three evaluators for every three portfolios being evaluated. Each portfolio will take approximately 45 minutes to thoroughly review and rate. Each oral presentation will take approximately one hour. For example, if there are 15 portfolios to be evaluated, you will need at least five panels of three evaluators—15 ratings total. Each panel of evaluators will rate three different portfolios or three different oral presentations. The ideal scenario is to have each portfolio evaluated by two different panels of evaluators (six different individuals). And, if possible, have two different panels hear each simulated-hearing presentation.

Collect all the judges' rating sheets at the conclusion of the portfolio or hearing evaluation. To determine the level of achievement for each portfolio or simulated hearing, combine individual evaluators' ratings then divide by the number of individual judges. This average rating will give you a number that you can use for determining different levels of achievement for the classes participating in the portfolio showcase or simulated hearing.

Continued on the Next Page →

The Center for Civic Education recommends the following rating ranges for determining the level of achievement:

Level of Achievement	Average Rating
Superior	50–41
Exceptional	40–31
Outstanding	30–21
Honorable Mention	20 or Below

For example, a portfolio or hearing might be rated as follows:

Rater	Average Rating		
Rater 1	38 points		
Rater 2	36 points	Total = 114 points	114 total points ÷ 3 = 38 (Exceptional)
Rater 3	40 points		

After the Evaluations

Hold an assembly of all participants, their teachers, families, and friends to notify them of the showcase results. The Center for Civic Education encourages educators to give each participating student a Certificate of Achievement with their name on it and have it signed by a community leader, such as a school administrator or elected public official.

If possible, arrange for a prominent community leader to present the Certificates of Achievement or any other awards, and give a brief address about the importance of the students' contributions and their policymaking achievement—a necessary step in maintaining a healthy democracy.

Evaluator Guidelines for the Portfolio Showcase

The Project Citizen portfolio showcase is the culmination of an interactive civic education program designed to actively engage adolescents in the civic life of their communities.

In Project Citizen, a group of participating young people identifies and analyzes issues and problems facing their community, their school, neighborhood, town, city, or state. As a group, students select one of these issues or problems for detailed study. After students complete their research, they propose a public policy to deal with that issue or problem. Finally, they develop an engagement plan specifying the steps to take to have their public policy proposal adopted by the appropriate government authorities.

To develop the Project Citizen portfolio, the students or youth-organization members are subdivided into four groups, one group for each section of the portfolio. Each group has responsibility for the following primary tasks:

- **Portfolio Group 1: Explaining the Problem**
- **Portfolio Group 2: Evaluating Alternative Policies to Deal With the Problem**
- **Portfolio Group 3: Proposing a Public Policy to Deal With the Problem**
- **Portfolio Group 4: Developing an Engagement Plan**

The class develops a portfolio based on their research. The portfolio has two components: a display component and a documentation component. The two components taken together constitute the portfolio that you will evaluate using the Portfolio Criteria Checklist and the Project Citizen Portfolio and Hearing Evaluation Rating Sheet—one section for each of the four sections of the display and documentation elements, and one for an overall evaluation of the students' work. The following information corresponds to the four major sections that comprise the display component and the documentation requirements.

Note: Students and their portfolio groups do not need to create physical posters as many project portfolios are presented digitally. The highlighted poster sections are merely illustrated to foster understanding of the differences between each section.

Continued on the Next Page →

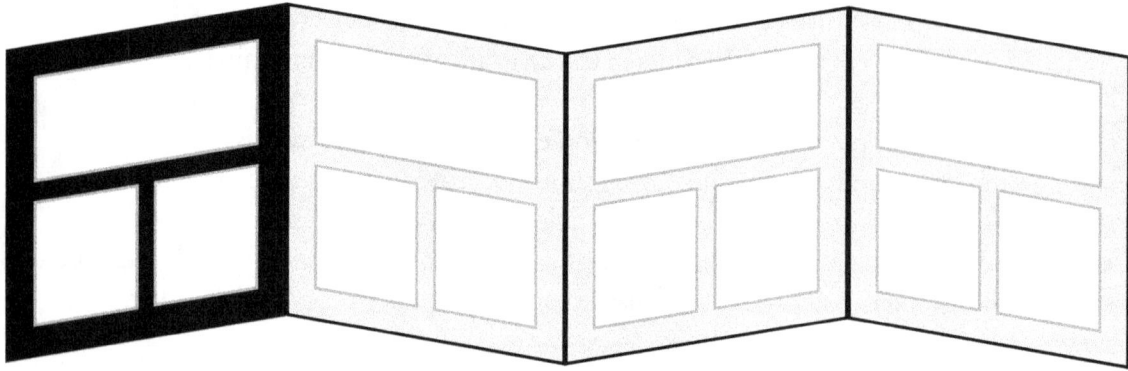

Portfolio Group 1: Explaining the Problem

The first display section should provide a detailed explanation of the issue or problem chosen and why the class selected it. A one- to two-page written summary should include a clear description of the issue or problem and what the class learned about it. Relevant graphs, photos, illustrations, or cartoons should be included. The students should cite all sources they used, all of which should be cited in the annotated bibliography for documentation.

The written summary should be part of the display and should include the following information:

- A clear statement of the nature of the issue or problem the students chose to research
- The degree of seriousness and scope of the issue or problem
- The levels of government or government agencies that have responsibility for handling the issue or problem
- An indication of individuals or groups that might share responsibility for dealing with the issue or problem
- An indication of disagreements about the issue or problem in the community
- Adequacy of existing policy, if applicable. (Why or why not?)

Documentation: In the first section, the students must document their research in the annotated bibliography. Documentation for this section should also include any additional evidence that supports the group's work.

Examples:
- The completed Graphic Organizer: Creating Solutions in the student edition
- A summary of the completed interviews (or representative examples)
- Relevant news articles
- Screenshots or digital images of evidence from the internet
- Other relevant supporting articles, reports, etc.

Continued on the Next Page →

Portfolio Group 2: Evaluating Alternative Policies to Deal With the Problem

The second display section should provide a detailed explanation and evaluation of two or three alternative public policy proposals from various groups or individuals. If an existing policy is in place, it should be included with an explanation of its effectiveness. Relevant graphs, photos, illustrations, or cartoons should be included. The students should cite all sources used.

The display should include a one-page written summary for each alternative public policy presented. Each summary should include the following information:

- An explanation of the current public policy, if one exists, and an evaluation of its effectiveness (advantages and disadvantages)
- A detailed explanation of each alternative public policy solution and its strengths and weaknesses (advantages and disadvantages) with supporting data
- Identification of the source of each proposed public policy (e.g., individual citizens, special-interest groups, legislature, or city council)

Documentation: In the second section of the documentation, the students must document their research, including a selection of the best supporting material. In addition to a table of contents, this section should include evidence that supports the group's work.

Examples:
- A copy of the full text of the policy (if one is currently in place)
- Messages or memos from special interest groups or individuals
- Publicity circulating in the community
- Other relevant supporting articles, reports, etc.

Continued on the Next Page →

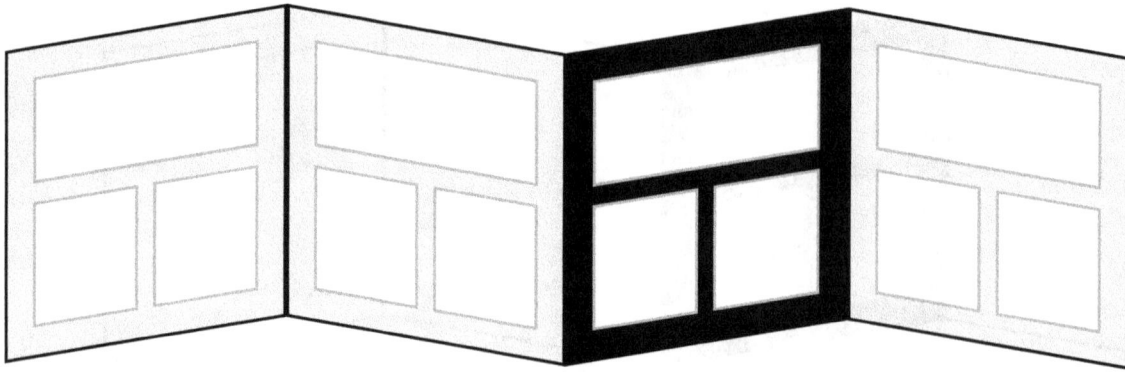

Portfolio Group 3: Proposing a Public Policy to Deal With the Problem

The third display section should clearly explain a specific public policy proposal to address the issue or problem and the reasons that the class has agreed to support it. The class may choose to support an existing policy, modify an existing policy, create a new policy, or support one of the alternative policies described in the second display panel. Graphs, photos, illustrations, or cartoons should be displayed. The students should cite all sources used.

The display should contain a one- to two-page written summary that includes the following:

- An explanation of the public policy the class is proposing and a justification for how that public policy will best deal with the issue or problem
- The advantages and disadvantages of the public policy supported with current data, including identification of individuals or groups that may be affected by the policy and a description of its possible impact
- A statement of rationale that also identifies the appropriate branch of government or governmental agency that would be responsible for implementing the proposed public policy
- An opinion statement on why the proposed public policy does not violate the U.S. Constitution or state constitutions

Documentation: In the third section of the documentation, students must document their research, including a selection of the best supporting material. This section should include evidence that supports the group's work.

Examples:
- A completed copy of the Graphic Organizer: Constitutional Opinion in the student edition
- Any laws, regulations, or rules that may apply
- A copy of an existing policy or law, or models of new or modified laws or policies
- Other relevant supporting articles, reports, etc.

Continued on the Next Page →

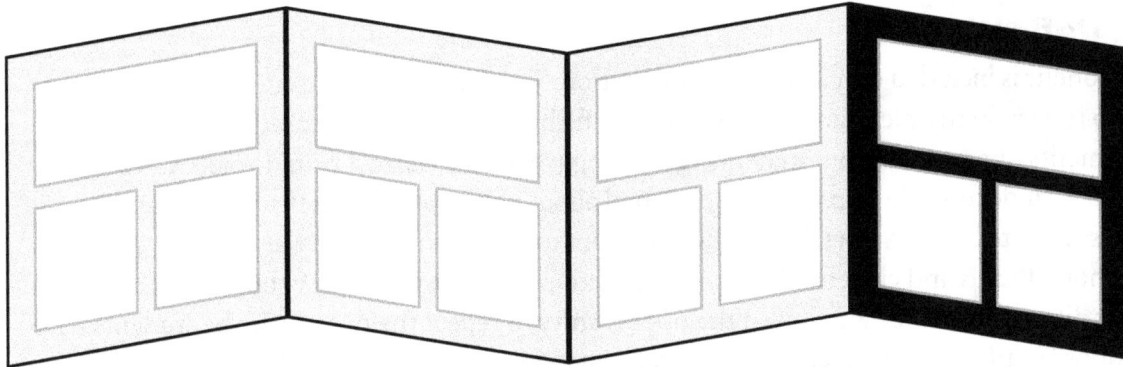

Portfolio Group 4: Developing an Engagement Plan

The fourth display section of the portfolio should provide a detailed description of the process necessary to get the proposed public policy adopted and implemented by the appropriate governmental branch or agency. The plan should include steps for developing community support for the proposed policy. There should also be a detailed plan for overall implementation of the proposed public policy. Graphs, photos, illustrations, or cartoons should be displayed. The students should cite all sources they used.

The following information should be included in the written summary:

- A clear explanation of how the class would seek to gain support from governmental officials for the proposed public policy
- A clear explanation of how the class would seek to gain support from special-interest groups, community groups, businesses, or influential individuals for the proposed public policy and engagement plan
- Identification of influential individuals, businesses, special-interest groups, or governmental agencies that might oppose the proposed public policy and engagement plan and an explanation of their opposition
- An explanation of steps to be taken to implement the engagement plan and the plan's benefits
- The estimated costs and a timeline for implementation of the engagement plan

Documentation: In the fourth section of documentation, the students must document their research, including a selection of the best supporting material. This section should include evidence that supports the group's work.

Examples:
- Written statements of support or opposition
- Publicity
- Messages from influential individuals or public officials
- Other relevant supporting articles, reports, etc.

Continued on the Next Page →

← **Continued From the Previous Page**

Part 5: Reflections

This component is included only in the documentation. The final step of the curriculum asks students to reflect on their learning experience. The fifth section of documentation should contain brief statements or messages from students describing what they learned from Project Citizen. This should include reflection on what they learned about public policy and the policymaking process. It should tell how Project Citizen helped them to better understand the role of governmental officials and citizens. Finally, the reflection should address how they would approach the project differently if they were given the opportunity to repeat the process. If the students have had an opportunity to present their portfolio to an audience in a simulated public hearing, they should include their thoughts on this experience in the reflection.

Project Citizen Portfolio and Hearing Evaluation Sheet

A Project Citizen portfolio consists of two components: a four-section display and an annotated bibliography. When evaluating the portfolio, the following criteria should be applied to both the display and the corresponding documentation.

Use this same sheet to evaluate the hearing or presentation of portfolios. The presentation will be made by four different groups of students, each presenting a different aspect of the entire group's research and its recommendation for a public policy. When evaluating each group, consider the criteria below for that group of students, and then use the following rating scale. Give only one whole numeric rating (1–10) for each of the five sections of the Criteria for Evaluation. Please also utilize the space in the margins for comments and suggestions.

Each portfolio section will receive a score of 1–10 (1 being the lowest and 10 being the highest). Points for each section will be distributed as Opportunities for Growth: 1–4, Meets Expectations: 5–6, and Exceeds Expectations: 7–10.

Continued on the Next Page →

1: Explanation of the Problem

Score:

Opportunities for Growth (1-4)	Meets Expectations (5-6)	Exceeds Expectations (7-10)

☐ Explains the problem, presents evidence of the problem, and names the problem's causes

☐ Demonstrates an understanding of issues involved in the problem

☐ Demonstrates an understanding of existing or proposed public policies that address the problem

☐ Explains disagreements about the problem that exist in the community

☐ Explains why government should be involved in the solution to the problem

☐ Presents mutually supporting information in the display, annotated bibliography, documentation binder, or digital format

2: Analysis of Alternative Policies

Score:

Opportunities for Growth (1-4)	Meets Expectations (5-6)	Exceeds Expectations (7-10)

☐ Presents two or three alternative public policies to address the problem

☐ Explains advantages and disadvantages of each alternative policy presented

☐ Identifies controversies and conflicts that may need to be addressed for each alternative

☐ Presents mutually supporting information in the display, annotated bibliography, documentation binder, or digital format

3: Public Policy Development and Persuasiveness

Opportunities for Growth (1-4)	Meets Expectations (5-6)	Exceeds Expectations (7-10)	Score:

☐ States a public policy that addresses the problem and identifies the governmental branch or agency responsible for enacting the proposed public policy

☐ Supports the proposed public policy with sound reasoning and evidence

☐ Identifies and explains advantages and disadvantages of the proposed public policy

☐ Explains the reasons why the proposed public policy is constitutional

☐ Presents mutually supporting information in the display, annotated bibliography, documentation binder, or digital format

4: Implementation of Engagement Plan

Opportunities for Growth (1-4)	Meets Expectations (5-6)	Exceeds Expectations (7-10)	Score:

☐ Identifies individuals and groups, both supporters and opponents, who will need to be influenced

☐ Identifies government officials, both supporters and opponents, who will need to be influenced

☐ Outlines and explains an action process for getting the proposed public policy enacted

☐ Proposes action that builds and expands on evidence presented in previous panels

☐ Presents mutually supporting information in the display, annotated bibliography, documentation binder, or digital format

5: Overall

Score: ___

Opportunities for Growth (1-4)	Meets Expectations (5-6)	Exceeds Expectations (7-10)

☐ Presents mutually supportive material in the display, annotated bibliography, documentation binder, or digital format

☐ Constructs a clear and convincing sequence from one section of the portfolio to the next

☐ Uses and documents research from multiple sources and provides appropriate citations for the sources and evidence used

☐ Uses standards of good writing

☐ Uses relevant and appropriate graphics and written information

☐ Is visually appealing

☐ Includes evidence of student reflection stating what students have learned

Total Score

Score: ___

(Sum of scores in all five categories)

Additional Notes Below

Evaluator Guidelines for the Simulated Hearing

The Project Citizen simulated hearing is the culmination of an interactive civic education program designed to actively engage young people in the civic life of their communities.

In Project Citizen, a group of participating young people identifies and analyzes issues and problems facing their community, their school, neighborhood, town, city, or state. As a group, students select one of these issues or problems for detailed study. After students complete their research, they propose a public policy to deal with that issue or problem. Finally, they develop an engagement plan specifying the steps to take to have their public policy proposal adopted by the appropriate government authorities.

The purpose of the simulated hearing (the oral-presentation component) is to teach students to present and defend reasoned opinions related to public policy decision-making in their communities.

For the simulated hearing, the class or youth-organization members are subdivided into four groups, one group for each section of the portfolio. Each group has responsibility for the following primary task:

- **Portfolio Group 1: Explaining the Problem**
- **Portfolio Group 2: Evaluating Alternative Policies to Deal With the Problem**
- **Portfolio Group 3: Proposing a Public Policy to Deal With the Problem**
- **Portfolio Group 4: Developing an Engagement Plan**

Each group will make a prepared four-minute presentation. The group will then respond for six minutes to follow-up questions posed by you and the other members of the evaluator panel. Each of the four groups will address your panel for a total of 10 minutes. At the conclusion of each presentation, you and the other panel members should provide constructive feedback.

The following information has been prepared to assist you in asking follow-up questions to each of the four groups. Please remember that these questions are suggested only as a guide to help you elicit additional information or elaborate on information presented in the testimony.

The goals of the follow-up period and guiding questions are to help you determine how much the students have learned about the problem they have investigated as well as the information-gathering and problem-solving process they have used. The more you learn about what the students have studied and proposed, the better you will be able to evaluate their presentation.

The following information has been prepared to assist you in evaluating the presentation of each of the four portfolio groups. The portfolio has two components: a display component and a documentation component. The two components taken together constitute the portfolio.

Continued on the Next Page →

The prepared statements and answers to your follow-up questions will be based on the portfolio. You will evaluate the student presentation using the five sections of the Project Citizen Portfolio and Hearing Evaluation Sheet—one for each of the four sections of the portfolio and one for an overall evaluation of the students' presentations.

Portfolio Group 1: Explaining the Problem

Portfolio Group 1 should provide a detailed explanation of the issue or problem chosen by the class and why that particular issue or problem was selected. During the prepared testimony phase, the group should be able to provide a detailed description of the problem's scope and impact on the community. Possible follow-up questions might include the following:

- How widespread is this issue or problem in your community?
- Is this an issue or problem that people in your community think is important? How do you know?
- What has public reaction to the issue or problem been?
- What sources of information did you use to research the issue or problem?
- What more did you learn about the issue or problem as a result of your research?
- What branch of government do you think should be dealing with the issue or problem and why?
- Are there policies, regulations, ordinances, or rules in place now that address the issue or problem? Do you believe they are adequate to deal with the issue or problem? Why or why not?

Portfolio Group 2: Evaluating Alternative Policies to Deal With the Problem

Portfolio Group 2 should focus on explaining existing or alternative policies designed to solve the problem or address the issue. In some instances, no policy exists, so students are expected to develop public policy alternatives to address the problem.

Testimony should include strengths and weaknesses of existing or proposed policies. Where no policy exists, students should explain what alternative policy proposals may be pending or recommended by their classmates, community groups, special-interest groups, formal boards, the legislature, or city councils. Advantages and disadvantages of each policy or proposal should be presented and discussed. Possible follow-up questions might include the following:

- What sources did you use to locate existing or proposed policies?
- What more did you learn about the issue or problem after you examined alternative policies?
- If a public policy currently exists, why does it need to be changed?
- Which groups or individuals support the existing policy or proposed policy, and what are the reasons for their support?

Continued on the Next Page →

← Continued From the Previous Page

- Which groups or individuals oppose changing the policy or proposed policy, and what are the reasons for their opposition?
- Were there other policies or solutions that you did not include in your portfolio or in your presentation? If so, what were they?

Portfolio Group 3: Proposing a Public Policy to Deal With the Problem

Portfolio Group 3 should focus on the policy or solution being proposed by the class. The group's explanation should include a clear rationale for making changes to existing policy, eliminating existing policy, or implementing new policy. If appropriate, students should present a cost analysis. The group must include an explanation of why its proposed policy does not violate the federal or state constitutions. Possible follow-up questions might include the following:

- What branch or agency of government is the proposed policy directed toward and why?
- Have you considered the total cost of implementing your policy? Why or why not? If you have, what is the total cost and what does it include?
- Where would the funds come from? What other resources besides money might be needed?
- Does the civil community or private sector (business) have any responsibility to correct the problem or to assist in carrying out the proposed public policy?

Portfolio Group 4: Developing an Engagement Plan

Portfolio Group 4 should focus on giving a detailed explanation of the steps needed to have the proposed policy adopted by the appropriate government officials. Testimony should include a statement on how long it might realistically take to get the proposed policy adopted and implemented. Possible follow-up questions might include the following:

- How could the groups or individuals who support your proposal help influence or convince government officials to adopt your proposal?
- Are there other individuals or groups who might support your recommended solution or policy? Why would they support your recommended solution or policy?
- What individuals or groups oppose your recommended solution or policy, and what are the reasons for their opposition?
- How would you respond to the arguments of the individuals or groups that are opposed to your policy?
- How long would it take to implement the proposal?
- What results would you expect if you carried out your engagement plan?
- What do you think might happen if your proposal were not adopted?

Continued on the Next Page →

← **Continued From the Previous Page**

General Questions

If appropriate, these generic questions might be asked of any of the four groups: "How does the [law or legal case] you mentioned in your testimony support your position? What did you learn about the role of government officials by participating in Project Citizen? What did you learn about the issues or problems facing your community by participating in Project Citizen?"

Feedback

The simulated hearing component of Project Citizen is an extension of classroom learning. As such, it presents another opportunity for you to help students understand the complexity of the public policymaking process. After each group presents its section of the portfolio, you are expected to provide the students with feedback on their presentation. These remarks should be short but constructive. You should commend the students for their work and help them learn from the process.

Always begin with positive remarks and add helpful examples of how the students might improve their presentation. For example, you might say, "I liked the way you explained the problem. I would like to suggest that you include more data on the number of people affected by this serious problem."

Some students will undoubtedly make errors in their presentation. During the feedback session, please make the correction in a tactful, sensitive, and diplomatic manner. For example, "Your presentation included an important reference to the Supreme Court's ruling in *New Jersey v. T.L.O.* That case relates to the Fourth Amendment's prohibition of unlawful search and seizure. Because your presentation focused on free speech, you might think about using the *Tinker v. Des Moines* case instead."

Evaluator Message

Dear [Name],

Thank you for your willingness to participate in the Project Citizen showcase. Your presence at the event will demonstrate the characteristics associated with civic duty and public commitment that is the desired outcome of the program. Project Citizen is designed to help promote competent and responsible participation in local, state, and federal government. The program helps young people learn how to monitor and influence public policy. In the process, they develop an understanding of democratic principles and gain faith in their ability to make a difference in their community.

Small groups of students work cooperatively to identify a public policy problem or issue in their community. They then research the problem, evaluate different solutions, develop a solution in the form of a public policy, and create an engagement plan to gain support from government authorities to adopt their proposed policy. In the showcase event, you will see and hear the work that students have undertaken to address a public policy issue facing their community.

There are two components of the showcase: (1) a review of the portfolio that the class has developed to present its research on the problem it is addressing and (2) a simulated hearing that is intended to represent the atmosphere of a public hearing before the governmental body or agency that would normally deal with the specific problem the students are addressing.

Component parts of the Project Citizen display and oral presentations include the following:

- **The Problem**
  - Explains a current public policy problem or issue, the policy currently in place for dealing with this problem, and why the current policy should be changed

- **Alternative Policies**
  - Analyzes two or three different policies or proposals for solving the problem
  - Explains advantages and disadvantages of each

- **Our Policy**
  - Outlines the group's chosen policy that it believes will best solve the problem
  - Justifies this policy as realistic, economically feasible, and constitutional

- **Engagement Plan**
  - Identifies specific stakeholders (supporters and opponents) who will be affected by this policy
  - Proposes actions the group will take to gain their support or persuade them that this is a sound policy choice

Continued on the Next Page →

We have included documents that will help you with your assignment for the showcase:

- Evaluator Guidelines for the Portfolio Showcase
- Project Citizen Portfolio and Hearing Evaluation Rating Sheet

Please review these materials before the event. We will hold a briefing session just prior to the start of the evaluation process to explain procedures for the event and to answer any questions that you may have.

Please remember that the focus of this project is to instill the civic skills and responsibilities our democracy requires by getting young people to participate in their own governance. As leaders and role models for these students, we hope you will support, encourage, and teach them how to be meaningful members of their communities, even if that requires discussing challenges to our current policies.

Finally, some of our students have accommodations that will support them during the hearing. This means that some of our students will have interpretation services available, assistive technology devices and software, and/or use nonverbal communication strategies, such as American Sign Language. We ask that you are aware that students will respond in the format that makes the most sense to them.

Yours truly,

[Teacher's Name]

For more information about Project Citizen, visit **civiced.org/project-citizen**.

APPENDIX C
MEDIA-LITERACY AND PUBLIC POLICY LESSONS

Media Literacy Lessons to Support Project Citizen

Throughout the Project Citizen student edition, you will notice callout sections titled "Media Literacy Moments." Each of these sections start with a compelling question that can drive student development of media-literacy skills. To bolster the content in those sections, there are eight media-literacy lessons and ancillary materials based on those compelling questions. To access these lessons and the associated ancillary materials, please go to civiced.org/pc2/lessonplans. Upon visiting that link, use the passcode "pcteacherguide" to access the media literacy lessons.

In each lesson you will find a short animated video to launch engagement on the compelling question, graphic organizers, presentation slides, and even games to support students as they navigate the media environment. Ideally, these lessons are to support the construction of a project for Project Citizen, but these lessons can also be used independent from the curriculum.

To see where a teacher might utilize each one of these lessons in conjunction with the student edition for Project Citizen, please see "Media Literacy in Project Citizen" in the front matter of this book.

The titles of each lesson are below.

Lesson	Media-Literacy Lessons	Project Citizen Curriculum Alignment
1	Does a Free Press Support Democracy?	Chapter 1
2	Do I Have a Role in Media Literacy?	Chapter 3, Steps 1 and 2
3	Is All Media Biased?	Chapter 3, Step 3
4	Can I Identify Reliable Media Sources?	Chapter 3, Step 3
5	Do I Play a Role in Staying Safe Online?	Chapter 3, Step 3
6	Do I Have to Cite My Sources?	Chapter 3, Step 4
7	Can I Effectively Create and Share Information?	Chapter 3, Step 4
8	Am I Media Literate?	Chapter 3, Step 6; Chapter 4

www.ingramcontent.com/pod-product-compliance
Lightning Source LLC
Chambersburg PA
CBHW080646270326

41928CB00017B/3212